Home Sweet Home
Augusta, Georgia

Mark Woodard

ISBN:1508491070
ISBN-13:9781508491071

DEDICATION

I dedicate this book to my wonderful wife, Lucinda,

Our four great children and their spouses:

Marie and William Hughes,

Joel and Amy Woodard,

Ben and Debbie Woodard,

Jon and Erin Woodard

And

Our twelve grandchildren.

CONTENTS

JAMES EDWARD OGLETHORPE

James Edward Oglethorpe, the father of Georgia, was born in London, England on December 22, 1696. Jamie, as he was called, didn't remember a lot about his father. His father died when Jamie was five years old. The

job of raising James and his six siblings fell on his mother, Lady Eleanor Oglethorpe. Eleanor loved her children and gave them her best.

James attended school at Eaton and Oxford and was elected to the British Parliament in 1722. In Parliament, he headed a committee looking into the debtors prisons –a prison dedicated solely to those unable to pay their debts. He found terrible things going on and ill practices within the prisons through his investigations. He had a friend, Robert Castel, who was a well-to-do architect who had been thrown into prison because he was unable to meet the demands of his creditors. The young man died while in prison.

In 1732, King George II granted a charter for another colony in America, which would later become the state of Georgia. It was the last of the original 13 Colonies. Oglethorpe asked Parliament to make Georgia a debtor's colony. Parliament said no to this proposal indicating that debtors would remain in prison in England. Parliament did, however, help people with no money that were willing and able to work cross the ocean and come to Georgia. In January of 1733, James Oglethorpe and 120 colonists arrived in America. They settled in this new country where the city of Savannah now stands.

In 1736, Roger Lacy and Kennedy O'Brian were sent out by Oglethorpe to establish a front door to the back country. The two men traveled up the Savannah River and chose the site where Fort Augusta was built. Oglethorpe knew that whoever controlled the Indian trade would control the Indians. This would be a major advantage in the years to come.

In 1735, Parliament passed several laws for Georgia. In order to hunt or trap animals in Georgia, one must have a Georgia license. When the license was secured, one must also post bond money in case the Indians filed a complaint against you. The law also stated that no other state license would suffice in place of one from Georgia. If you were caught without a license you would be fined. Another Act imposed by Parliament was the "No Rum Act." The Carolinians had been trading rum for deer skins and the Indians felt they had been made drunk and then cheated. Oglethorpe put an end to this with the "No Rum Act." In addition to this Act, in 1735, slaves were forbidden in Georgia with the "No Slave Act." The Spaniards, who tried to claim Georgia, had settled in Florida and the fear was if the Spaniards and Indians of Florida were to attack Georgia the slaves might join them. In 1742, the Spanish did attack Georgia but were unsuccessful. The "No Slave Act" was repealed and the decision was made in 1749 to allow slaves in Georgia.

Fort Augusta was big in Indian trading. Oglethorpe did not want the Indians to come to Augusta, but rather for the traders to go to the Indians to trade goods. The traders would pack all their trading items on mules or horses, put bright ribbons in their manes, and bells around their necks. You could hear them coming a mile away. The longest recorded horse train was approximately 200 horses. James Edward was a good man and a great leader. He spent 91,705 lbs. of his own money to establish the colony of Georgia and for that Georgians are thankful. He set sail for England, arriving in London on September 28, 1743. He lived out the remainder of his life there, dying on June 30, 1785.

Research sources:

1. *The Story of Augusta. Cashin, Edward J. Spartanburg, SC. The Reprint Company Publishing. (1996)*
2. *Augusta, A Pictorial History. Callahan, Helen. Richmond County Historical Society Publisher. (1980)*
3. *Confederate City, Augusta Georgia 1860-1865. Corley, Florence Fleming. (1995)*
4. *Memorial History of Augusta, Georgia. Jones, Charles C. Spartanburg, SC. The Reprint Publishers. (1890)*
5. *James Edward Oglethorpe. Blackburn, Joyce. Mockingbird Books. (1970)*

AUGUSTA, GEORGIA

As times change, names change. For example, the Savannah River hasn't always been called the Savannah River and was once known as the

Westobu River, named after the Westos Indians. The Westos Indians lived on either side of the river and were not well liked among the other Indian tribes because they were cannibalistic. At times they would eat their enemies as a show of power! They were finally beaten in war and those few remaining Westos Indians became a part of the Creek Nation.

The city of Augusta also has an interesting story behind its name. Years ago in England, in 1735, King George II was on the throne. He had three daughters and a son, Frederick Louis, Prince of Wales. In 1733, the famous artist, Mercer, painted a picture of the four children in a portrait called the "Music Party." They all looked so happy playing their instruments, but that was not the case. Frederick didn't get along with his sisters, or maybe they didn't get along with him and the siblings were anything but happy. Frederick was

approaching the age to marry and unlike today, the father would choose the bride for his son. So Frederick went to his father, King George II and the King wrote a friend to see if his daughter would marry his son. The wedding was set for 1736. They weren't sure the bride would show up, but she did. The bride was Princess Augusta of Saxe-Gotha. Fredrick and Augusta were married and many said she was gangly and somewhat awkward, but Augusta was a good wife. She didn't care about politics and took good care of her family. Prince Frederick never became King of England, but he and Augusta had a child that did, eventually becoming King George III in 1760. When Frederick and Augusta were married, James Edward Oglethorpe decided to name the Fort for her. Fort Augusta eventually became a town and now a city and has carried her name for over 250 years. A fort was also named for Prince Fredrick down on the coast, Fort Frederica.

King George III was 22 when he ascended to the throne. It's interesting to note that as a young man, King George III's heart was touched by the fifteen year old daughter of the Duke of Richmond. Richmond County was named for him. King George III was on the throne when the Americans had become tired of England's intervention and decided to declare their independence. On July 4, 1776 the "Declaration of Independence" was signed and given to King George, solidifying America's independence from England. Many English traditions and connections remain, however, including the name Augusta from Princess Augusta of Saxe-Gotha.

Research sources:

1. *The Story of Augusta. Cashin, Edward J. Spartanburg, SC. The Reprint Company Publishing. (1996)*
2. *Augusta, A Pictorial History. Callahan, Helen. Richmond County Historical Society Publisher. (1980)*
3. *Confederate City, Augusta Georgia 1860-1865. Corley, Florence Fleming. (1995)*
4. *Memorial History of Augusta, Georgia. Jones, Charles C. Spartanburg, SC. The Reprint Publishers. (1890)*
5. *From City to Countryside. Haltermann, Bryan M. (1997)*
6. *Articles from the Augusta Chronicle.*

ST. PAUL'S EPISCOPAL CHURCH

St. Paul's was the first church built in Augusta back in 1750. The city trustees got together and decided if Augusta was going to be a proper town they needed a church. In 1750 they built the building but they

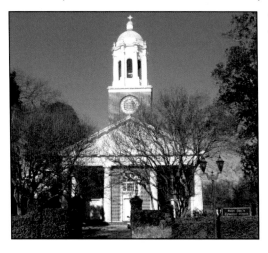

didn't have a preacher so the trustees wrote the Church of England asking for a rector or a pastor. The Church of England sent over Mr. Jonathan Copp and he and his family arrived in Augusta in 1751. Jonathan Copp brought a gift with him, a baptismal font from St. Paul's Church in England. Jonathan Copp

did not like Augusta because he felt it was too much of an Indian town and he was fearful of the Indians, especially the tradition of scalping. Rector Copp wrote back to England asking if he and the family could come home, but the Church said no and they said it would do him good if he

stayed. Poor Jonathan Copp stayed five years and was then finally transferred down to Savannah, scalp and all.

St. Paul was built for protection next to Fort Augusta. It was a small clapboard building and was the only church in Augusta for several years. Different denominations used the

building. The Presbyterians used St Paul's until their building was built in 1804. St. Paul's first building stood until 1781, when it was destroyed during the last battle in Augusta in the Revolutionary War. The Colonists were fighting against British Colonel Thomas Brown in Fort Cornwallis. Brown surrendered along with 300 British troops, but during the battle the church was destroyed. The trustees of Richmond County built a second clapboard building to replace the one destroyed.

The members of St. Paul's Episcopal Church in Augusta, decided it was time to have a brick building, so in 1820, they built it. By this time there were plenty of churches in Augusta, but the members of St. Paul felt their Church was special.

The third building, a brick church, sat on the same spot for 96 years. In March of 1916, a fire broke out at the Dyer building at the corner of Broad and Eighth Street. It was very windy and burning wood was flying through the air. The Chronicle Newspaper initially reported 25 city blocks were burned. They later reported it had actually been 32 city blocks. St. Paul's Church burned that night along with Tubman High School for Girls, many businesses and houses. During the fire a young man, a member of the church, ran into the building. He could see people taking things. With a loud voice he yelled trying to sound as low as he could, "That's not yours. It belongs to God." The men dropped what they had and took off. The young man was able to grab and carry only one thing out of the building, the baptismal font, the gift originally from St. Paul's in England back in 1751. The baptismal font was the only thing saved in the 1916 city fire. The church was once again rebuilt in 1918 and today it looks very much like the Church of 1820, only a little bigger. In the foyer you'll see the 1751 baptismal font; you'll also see a painting of William Few, signer of the Constitution. Few is buried outside in the church yard. It's a wonderful structure and worth seeing. A bronze plaque, dedicated too Richard Tubman, was destroyed in the 1916 city fire. The body of Richard Tubman is buried in a crypt below St. Paul's Episcopal Church.

If you drive by during the day, you'll notice the front door is left open. Visitors are welcome to stop inside and step into a piece of Augusta's history book.

Research resources:

1. *The Story of Augusta. Cashin, Edward J. Spartanburg, SC. The Reprint Company Publishing. (1996)*
2. *Augusta, A Pictorial History. Callahan, Helen. Richmond County Historical Society Publisher. (1980)*
3. *Memorial History of Augusta, Georgia. Jones, Charles C. Spartanburg, SC. The Reprint Publishers. (1890)*
4. *From City to Countryside. Haltermann, Bryan M. (1997)*
5. *Colonial Augusta, "Key to the Indian Country", Cashin, Edward J. Mercer University Press, Macon Georgia. (1986)*
6. *"A Tour of Saint Paul's Episcopal Church and Its Grounds in Augusta Georgia", A brochure. (2002)*

THOMAS BROWN

Thomas Brown is a name that can bring cold shivers to people living in Augusta. Thomas Brown was born on May 27, 1750, in Whitley of Yorkshire. His dad was Jonas Brown and his mother, Margaret Jackson Brown. Jonas Brown was a ship owner and conducted business around the world. Thomas had the chance to meet adventurer James Cook in 1771 while he was transacting business for his father in Nova Scotia, New England, the Carolinas, and Barbados.

In 1774, Thomas moved to Georgia and became the next door neighbor to Daniel Marshall, the great pioneer preacher of the "Separate Baptist Movement." Marshall arrived in what is today called Appling, but then was known as Brownsboro. Daniel Marshall erected the first Baptist church building in Georgia and it still stands today near Appling.

Now Brown came to Georgia when the back country was all upset. In fact on August 2, 1775, Thomas Brown was made an object lesson by the "Sons of Liberty." Brown was staying at his friend's house, James Gordon, in Richmond County when approximately one hundred Liberty Boys called on him, asking him to sign a document upholding the Association. Thomas Brown came out on the porch and said "no", because he was an Englishman who stood behind King George. With guns drawn, he fired his pistols. The first pistol misfired, but the second pistol did not. He shot the leader of the mob, Chesley Bostick, through his foot. About that time Brown was hit in the head with a rifle butt. In a semi-conscious state he was carried off to Augusta. Later, in a letter to his dad, he said that he was tied to a tree and fire branded. They took branches, set them on fire and held them under his feet and he was then tar and feathered. Thomas said he could not walk properly for several months and that he lost two toes that night. He was mad and was determined he would make them pay.

In 1780, Thomas Brown of Fort Cornwallis, the name of the new fort which stood where Fort Augusta had stood before, was on his way back with his British troops. A local town's person, Elijah Clark, was waiting for him. He attacked Brown, along with his men and 300 Indians. They fought the best they could, but finally they took cover in the old McKay Trading Post, (not the Ezekiel Harris house). Elijah Clark could not over power them and Thomas Brown couldn't fight his way out, but one British soldier managed to escape and went over to Ninety-Six, South Carolina, to the British Fort. Things in Ninety-Six were bad - water had been cut off so the only thing the British had to drink was their urine and all they had to eat were raw pumpkins. After five days, with no food or water, about the time the British were becoming weak, word came that help was on the way. British reinforcements were seen crossing the river and Elijah Clark and his men quickly broke camp and ran. They fought the British all the way up Battle Row.

Meanwhile, back in Augusta, some of Clark's men didn't know what was happening, but before long they were captured. Thomas Brown ordered thirteen of the men hung from the stairwell of his home so he could lie in his bed and watch them die. Brown had been wounded in the fight and the rest of the men the British captured were turned over to the Indians to be tortured and killed. That's why the name Thomas Brown brings cold shivers to Augustans – the tales of his ruthless punishment for these brave men seeking liberty still endure and are well known in Augusta.

Research resources:

1. *The Story of Augusta. Cashin, Edward J. Spartanburg, SC. The Reprint Company Publishing. (1996)*
2. *Memorial History of Augusta, Georgia. Jones, Charles C. Spartanburg, SC. The Reprint Publishers. (1890)*
3. *The King's Ranger. Cashin, Edward J. (1990)*

ROBERT FORSYTH

Robert Forsyth was born in Scotland in 1754. He came to America with his parents and lived in New England. At some point, prior to his 20th birthday, he moved to Fredericksburg, Virginia.

When America went to war with England for independence, Forsyth fought in the Continental Army. Three years later, on January 10, 1779, he received a commission as Captain in the Core of Partisan Light Dragoons under Major "Light Horse Harry" Lee.

Robert Forsyth decided to leave Lee's Legion to accept another post. He received a letter from General George Washington expressing regret that he was leaving Lee's command, but relief that Forsyth would be "in another line of the Army." Working as aide-de-camp to General Avery, Forsyth's new responsibility was to provide provisions for the southern army and on March 21, 1781, Forsythe earned a promotion to Major of the first Virginia Legion.

After the war, Forsyth returned to Fredericksburg. He married and had two sons, Robert and John. In 1785 Forsyth and his family moved to Augusta, Georgia where he engaged in private business, real estate and farming. Forsyth was active in various civic affairs and served his community as a tax assessor and justice of the peace. Forsyth became a trustee of Richmond Academy, a member of the Society of the Cincinnati and the Masons. He also became Master of the Lodge in Columbia and

Deputy Grand Master for the state of Georgia.

In 1789, President George Washington appointed him as the first Marshal for the District of Georgia. Robert Forsyth conducted his first U.S. census in 1790 and on January 11, 1794, Marshal Forsyth, accompanied by two of his deputies, went to the house of Mrs. Dixon in Augusta to serve a civil court process on two brothers, Beverly and William Allen. Beverly Allen, a former Methodist minister from South Carolina, saw the Marshal approaching and hid in a room on the second floor of the house. When Forsyth knocked on the door of the room, Alan fired his pistol at the direction of the knocking. The ball hit Forsyth in the head, killing him

instantly. The deputies arrested the two brothers immediately. Robert Forsyth was 40 years old and left behind a wife and two young sons, Robert and John. John was 13 at the time of his father's death. William Allen pleaded not guilty and was released on bail. Beverly Allen was sent to the Richmond County Jail, but managed to escape with the help of a guard. He was recaptured a short time later and placed in the Albert County, Georgia jail. Justice was not to be served, however. Led by William Allen, a group of armed men helped Beverly Allen escape the second time. The Allen Brothers reportedly fled to Texas and were never recaptured.

Robert Forsyth was buried at St. Paul's Episcopal Church Cemetery in Augusta Georgia. His grave is marked with a stone which reads:

Sacred to the memory of Robert Forsyth Federal Marshal of Georgia who, in the discharge of the duties of his office fell a victim to his respect for the laws of his Country and his resolution in support of them, on the 11th day of January 1794 in the 40 years of age. His virtues as an officer of rank and unusual competence in the war which gave independence to the United States and in all the tender and endearing relations of social life have left impressions on his Country and friends more durable engraved than this Monument. Marshal Forsyth was survived by his wife and their two sons, Robert and John. John Forsyth later became the governor of Georgia and the U.S. Minister to Spain, helping negotiate the treaty with Spain that acquired Florida for the United States.

In 1981 the United States Marshals Service created the "Robert Forsyth Act of Valor Award," which commemorates the first Marshal killed while performing the duties of his office. The award consists of a gold plaque and $1500, which is given to a U.S. Marshal Service employee who has demonstrated unusual courage, good judgment, and competence in hostile circumstances, or who has performed an act or service which saved the life of another person while endangering his/her own life.

Several years ago I was watching television as President George Bush Sr. addressed a group of law enforcement officials. He stated "that over the years we have lost (I don't remember the number) men and women who gave their lives in the line of duty starting with Robert Forsyth in Augusta, Georgia."

Research resources:

1. *The Lawman: US Marshals and Their Deputies, 1789-1989. Calhoun, Frederick. New York, Penguin Books. 1991*
2. *The History of the U.S. Marshals. Sumer, Robin Langley. Philadelphia, Courage Books. 1993*

MAYHAM TOWER

The year was 1781 and in late May, the British forces, under Lieutenant Col. Thomas Brown, controlled Fort Cornwallis. The fort was located about where St. Paul's Church now stands. The Colonial Troops had completely surrounded the fort, led by General Andrew Pickens and Lieutenant Colonel Henry, "Light Horse Harry" Lee. Colonel Henry Lee (father of the Civil War General, Robert E. Lee). The Americans were

unable to take the fort by force, however. This occurred before we had the levy which was built by the river. At that time the land sloped to the river and was flat and swampy. The men couldn't find a place to fire cannon balls over the walls of the fort, but then Colonel Lee suggested a strategy used a month before at Fort Wilson in South Carolina.

There, Major Hezekiah Mayham came up with the idea of building a tower that could be used to hoist cannons to the top, firing over the wall into the fort. In the writing of his memoirs Colonel Lee described the tower as "a large, strong, oblong pen. It was covered on the top with a floor of logs and protected on the side, opposite the fort, with a breastwork of light timber." The American leadership liked the idea and began building the tower on the evening of May 30, 1781. The tower was protected from British sight by a wooden house.

The tower was completed June 1, 1781. They put a six pounder cannon at the top and it was high enough to overlook the wall of Fort Cornwallis. British Colonel Brown recognized the danger of the tower so he ordered a night attack to destroy it. The Americans were able to repel their attack with bayonets, forcing Colonel Brown to use two cannons to fire at the tower. That's when the Americans opened fire from their cannon on the tower disabling the two cannons inside the fort. The Americans continued firing on the fort causing the British to dig holes in the ground to get out of the way of the shots. After a few days, the British had had enough and Colonel Thomas Brown sent word that he was ready to surrender. On June 5, the British troops stacked their arms in the fort and marched out of the gate between two lines of Colonial Soldiers. They were then taken into custody and a few months later, the British surrendered and America was free.

A lot of damage was done to the house during the battle and St. Paul's Church was completely destroyed. If you go to St. Paul's Church, pull into the parking lot and on the right you'll see the Celtic cross. At the foot of the Celtic cross you'll see one of the cannons used in the Battle of 1781. If you go back out to Reynolds Street, turn right, and go down a couple of blocks, you'll come to the Cotton Exchange Building on your right. Next to this building, you'll find a historical marker. The marker is the location of Mayham's Tower, giving Major Hezekiah Mayham credit for the victory in Augusta.

Research resources:

1. *The Story of Augusta. Cashin, Edward J. Spartanburg, SC. The Reprint Company Publishing. (1996)*
2. *Memorial History of Augusta, Georgia. Jones, Charles C. Spartanburg, SC. The Reprint Publishers. (1890)*

THE AUGUSTA CHRONICLE

Augusta is full of history, with many firsts. The first ice machine that came to America in 1863 came to Augusta, the Southern Baptist Convention started on Greene Street in Augusta in 1845, and Richmond Academy, the oldest chartered school in the south, started here in 1783.

The newspaper has quite a history, too. If you look at the front page at  the top, it says "Augusta Chronicle" and right below that it says, "The South's oldest newspaper established 1785." The Augusta Chronicle has had many different editors during its time in circulation and many of these men were quite interesting. The Augusta Chronicle was first printed on August 30, 1785 by Greenberg Hughes and was called the "Weekly Augusta Gazette." It was first printed in a building at the 300 block of 5th Street, and there is a historical marker at the site. The second owner and publisher, John Erdmann Smith, was a native of Germany. He promised to make the paper a place for free and ample discussion of political topics. The next editor and publisher remained true to the spirit. Patrick Walsh, a native Irishman, was owner and editor from 1880 to 1889. He also served at various times as Augusta's mayor, a City Councilman, a state Representative and a US Senator. Welch's statue now stands in Barrett Plaza on Telfair Street.

After the Civil War the editor of the paper wrote Sherman asking him why he had not burned Augusta. Sherman received the letter and sent one right back. "He said, he didn't think you would mind, but he could get the boys together and come back and burn the city, just let me know." Nothing else was ever said.

Thomas W. Loyless owned the newspaper from 1903 to 1919. In 1911, Loyless became the majority owner of the August Chronicle. He was a part of a group of investors that featured among them, Ty Cobb, the baseball legend. Three years later Loyless moved the newspaper into the city's first skyscraper. It was called the "Chronicle Building." Today it's called the Marian Building. It stands 10 stories high and was said to be fireproof. Two years later, during the city fire of 1916, the building was gutted. The Chronicle moved out of the building and never returned. They moved into a building right beside the Marian Building.

After Loyless was editor, Thomas J. Hamilton filled his seat. Hamilton published a column called, "Ambition for Augusta." In it, he wrote of Augusta's need for a power dam, an airfield, a city planning commission, hotels, a new black grammar school, and a University. Much of his vision became reality before his death in 1937.

The Chronicle's ownership entered the Morris family in 1945. William S. Morris Jr. and Henry A. Moore purchased a controlling interest. In 1955, Mr. Morris and his wife Florence Hill Morris bought Mr. Moore's share of stock. During the 1950s and early 1960s, the Chronicle Publishing Company grew becoming "The Southeastern Newspaper Corporation." In 1966 Morris's oldest son, William S. Morris III, took control. Under his leadership the company grew even more. In 1970 "Morris Communication" was formally founded.

Research resources:

1. *The Story of Augusta. Cashin, Edward J. Spartanburg, SC. The Reprint Company Publishing. (1996)*
2. *Augusta, A Pictorial History. Callahan, Helen. Richmond County Historical Society Publisher. (1980)*
3. *Confederate City, Augusta Georgia 1860-1865. Corley, Florence Fleming. (1995)*
4. *Memorial History of Augusta, Georgia. Jones, Charles C. Spartanburg, SC. The Reprint Publishers. (1890)*

SPRINGFIELD BAPTIST CHURCH

Over the years, here in Augusta, a wealth of notable history comes from African Americans like the start of Springfield Baptist Church, which dates

back to 1773. In 1773, three years before the "Declaration of Independence" was signed, David George, Jesse Peters Galphin and six other men formed the first permanent African American church at Silver Bluff, South Carolina. In 1778, the British invaded Silver Bluff. The masters and their slaves fled across the Savannah River into Georgia. In 1787, Springfield Baptist Church was organized on the site where it stands today.

Where did Springfield get its name? The area between Campbell's Gully and Hawks Gully was divided into six 50 acre grants under Oglethorpe's 1736 plan for Augusta. It was settled during the colonial period. The name Springfield first appeared on a plot of land west of Campbell's Gully in 1759. In time, the locals applied the name to the low-lying area between the two gullies.

As to the question which church was established first, the African American church in Savannah or Springfield Baptist? It was Springfield Baptist. In 1788, Jesse Peters Galphin and white Abraham Marshall from

Kiokee Baptist Church (the first Baptist Church in Georgia) ordained Andrew Bryan, founder of the first African American Church in Savannah. Meanwhile Rev. Seth Mead, pastor of St. John's Methodist Church, was building a wooden building on Greene Street, not too far from the horse racing track. The building was finished in 1801. The Methodists used the building until 1844, when they built the new brick building. In 1844, they sold the wooden building to Springfield Baptist. They rolled the building on logs from Greene Street to where the brick building of Springfield Baptist stands today. The 1801 wooden building sits beside the brick building. The old wooden building was used until 1897, when the church built a new brick edifice. The old wooden building was then moved back to its present location.

In 1859, Springfield Baptist Church established the first Negro Baptist Sunday School in Georgia and the entire United States. In 1866, the Georgia Equal Rights Association was organized here. In the year 1867, Morehouse College was founded in Springfield Baptist Church. It was first known as Augusta Baptist Institute. It started with 37 students in the basement of the 1801 church building, when it was setting where the brick building sits today. It started opening doors to an education once closed to blacks. Key in education at the time were William J. White and Simon Beard. A few years later, the school moved to Atlanta and in 1913 changed the name to Morehouse College.

Cedar Grove Cemetery was the first black cemetery in Augusta. It was started by Springfield Baptist Church and was named for all the cedar trees. The trees were all cut down and sold. In 1888 the church was declared free of all debts. In 1982 the 1801 building was officially listed in the National Registry of Historic Places. In 1989 the brick building was listed also. Springfield Baptist Church is a great part of Augusta's history. The building, built in 1801, is the oldest standing church building in Augusta. Be sure to go by and see the church located on the corner of Reynolds and 12th Street.

Research resources:

1. *The Story of Augusta. Cashin, Edward J. Spartanburg, SC. The Reprint Company Publishing. (1996)*
2. *Augusta, A Pictorial History. Callahan, Helen. Richmond County Historical Society Publisher. (1980)*
3. *Confederate City, Augusta Georgia 1860-1865. Corley, Florence Fleming. (1995)*
4. *Memorial History of Augusta, Georgia. Jones, Charles C. Spartanburg, SC. The Reprint Publishers. (1890)*
5. *From City to Countryside. Haltermann, Bryan M. (1997)*

MEADOW GARDEN

Meadow Garden, have you heard of it? Do you know where it's located?

Close to the canal on Thirteenth Street, you'll see the sign, Meadow Garden. It is located right in the middle of Walton Rehabilitation Center. The owners of the house, the "Daughters of the American Revolution," will tell you it's the oldest documented house in Augusta. The left side of the house is the oldest and was built by John Pettigru back in 1759 – only 23 years after Augusta was settled! Of course, the occupant of the house is what makes the house famous. George Walton was the youngest signer of the "Declaration of Independence." He was only 26 when he signed it. He was elected governor of Georgia in 1779 and was elected governor again in 1789. In October 1789 Walton accepted the

Constitution of the United States on behalf of the people of Georgia, becoming the fourth state to sign. Two months later, the state assembly elected him as Chief Justice in Georgia. In his new office, George Walton aided in the debate that indirectly ended up with a portion of Richmond County breaking away. William Few, who signed the Constitution of the United States for Georgia, named the new county calling it Columbia County. Walton was also appointed to the U.S. Senate from 1795 to 1796. George Walton and his wife Dorothy raised two sons in the house, Thomas and George Jr. In June of 1791 Walton acquired two adjacent lots. Each lot had 50 acres for a total of 100 acres. They were located in Augusta Township, outside of Augusta proper. At the time, it was all farmland and woods, a lot different than it looks today.

The left side of the house was built in 1759. George Walton was living on the property by early 1792 and chose to call the home Meadow Garden because the land had a large meadow on it. From 1790 to 1804 he would sign his correspondences, George Walton of Meadow Garden. Walton had financial troubles that never fully dissolved. Because he needed to ensure that his family would not be deprived of their home, he had the properties listed in the name of his nephew, Thomas Watkins and then later held in trust by John Habersham and Anderson Watkins for his son, George Walton Jr. The original house that Walton lived in had four rooms, two downstairs and two upstairs. You can still see where the ladder came up to the second floor. The second house, the house on the right, was joined to the original house in the very early 1800s. If you stand in the front yard and look at the house you'll notice the different levels of the windows. Once you go into the house you'll notice the two floor levels. You can still see where the two houses were joined together.

Thomas Walton died suddenly in December of 1803. His dad took the news hard. George Walton died two months later in February of 1804. The house did go to his son George Jr. It wasn't long before he and his family moved out of state. In 1900, the "Daughters of the American Revolution" bought the house. In 1901 they opened it for tours. If you haven't toured Meadow Garden you need to go. They are open Monday thru Friday. While you're there be sure to view the painting of George Washington. We're thrilled to have Meadow Garden in Augusta.

Research resources:

1. *The Story of Augusta. Cashin, Edward J. Spartanburg, SC. The Reprint Company Publishing. (1996)*
2. *Memorial History of Augusta, Georgia. Jones, Charles C. Spartanburg, SC. The Reprint Publishers. (1890)*
3. *From City to Countryside. Haltermann, Bryan M. (1997)*
4. *Haunted Augusta and Local Legends. Joiner, Sean. (2002)*

THE EZEKIEL HARRIS HOUSE

The Ezekiel Harris House at 1822 Broad Street is one of the oldest houses in Augusta, built in 1797 by Ezekiel Harris. The "Georgia Historical

Commission" purchased this house back in the 1950s. They thought they had purchased the "McKay Trading Post," which is where a battle was fought during the Revolutionary War in 1780. The much feared Colonel Thomas Brown of the British Army was marching back to Fort Cornwallis. Colonel Elijah Clarke and his men surprised Brown, surrounding him. Colonel Brown and his men, with some 300 Indians, took refuge in and around the Robert McKay Trading Post. On September 14, 1780, Elijah Clarke instructed his men to go down to the river and block the stream that brought fresh water to the McKay House.

After that action, the British weren't getting any water to drink. Elijah Clarke tried to overtake the house, but couldn't. During the battle Thomas Brown was wounded. After Brown realized he couldn't get away, he instructed one of his men to escape and go to the British Post at Ninety Six, South Carolina. Was Brown's man able to slip through the line and make it to Ninety Six? Brown's men were hungry and thirsty with nothing to drink. All they had to eat were raw pumpkins. Thomas Brown told his men to save their urine, they could drink that. To show he was serious, he was the first one to take a drink. Three days had gone by, and they were in bad shape. Someone noticed British reinforcement troops coming. The Colonial troops withdrew leaving about 30 wounded soldiers behind. Thirteen of the soldiers Brown hung on a stair rail so he could watch them die from his bed. The rest he gave to the Indians who slowly killed them. This all took place at the McKay Trading Post.

The "Georgia Historical Commission" thinking they had the McKay House, fully restored the house in 1964 listing it on the "National Register of

Historic Places." It was advertised as the "Shrine to the American Revolution." In the 1970s word came that this was not the McKay House but the Ezekiel Harris House. The McKay House was made of stone and was 80 yards from the river. The group that restored the house gave it to the city of Augusta. The house is made of wood even though brick was commonly used at the time. In September 1797, Harris announced in the Augusta Chronicle that his warehouse was prepared to receive tobacco and offered housing for planters. The announcement read, "A good farmhouse with a brick chimney will be ready by the first of January 1798."

The Ezekiel Harris house is now open as a museum. If you've been to the house you probably have seen the two rooms off the back porch. The house was built with no nails. It was pegged together with wooden pegs. Ezekiel Harris came to Augusta to set up a tobacco inspection center. There were 20 inspection centers in this area. Ezekiel Harris, along with his wife Eleanor and children lived in the house 10 years. During that time, he started the town of Harrisburg which is still there today. While the Harris' lived in the house, a daughter was born. In March of 1806 Eleanor died of breast cancer. Over the years, Ezekiel Harris had been taken to court over business dealings. When he lost in court, he would sell off part of his land for the money needed moving to Wilkes County in 1807. The Ezekiel Harris House built in 1798 stands as a rare example of the Georgian style of architecture, a style prominent in Colonial America. It also stands as a monument to the man who had it built.

Research resources:

1. *The Story of Augusta. Cashin, Edward J. Spartanburg, SC. The Reprint Company Publishing. (1996)*
2. *Augusta, A Pictorial History. Callahan, Helen. Richmond County Historical Society Publisher. (1980)*
3. *Confederate City, Augusta Georgia 1860-1865. Corley, Florence Fleming. (1995)*
4. *Memorial History of Augusta, Georgia. Jones, Charles C. Spartanburg, SC. The Reprint Publishers. (1890)*
5. *From City to Countryside. Haltermann, Bryan M. (1997)*
6. *Articles from the Augusta Chronicle.*

EMILY HARVEY THOMAS TUBMAN

She was born on March 21, 1794 when George Washington was our President. Her name was Emily Harvey Thomas and she was born in Ashland, Virginia. Her father's name was Edward Pendleton Thomas and her mother's name was Ann Chiles Thomas. Edward Thomas sold land in Kentucky before it became a state in 1792. Edward Thomas packed his family up and moved to the new capital of Kentucky, Frankfort. This land register had personally acquired more than 17,000 acres, but it ended when Edward suddenly died in 1803. Anne Thomas was left with five children. Emily, almost ten, was the oldest child. Before his death, Edward Thomas had worked it out with the great American orator and statesman Henry Clay that if something happened to him Henry Clay would become his children's

legal guardian. It was from the most picturesque section of Kentucky that Emily had her first memories. Emily lived a very secure life, thanks to her father, his money and preplanning. She did not attend school but must have had private tutoring.

By now you're probably asking, what has Emily Thomas got to do with Augusta? Well, Mr. And Mrs. Nicholas Ware, who lived in Augusta, invited a cousin of Mrs. Wares, Emily Thomas, to come and visit them. But Ann Thomas said she would not allow Emily to travel alone. So in the fall of 1818 Nicholas Ware went to Kentucky and brought Emily back to

Augusta. They rode horses and the return trip took two weeks. The Wares had invited Emily to visit them as a companion for their adopted daughter, Mary Ariuton Ware. When Emily came in 1818, she was 24 years old. Mary Ware was engaged to William White Holt. While Emily was visiting she met and fell in love with Richard C. Tubman. Richard Tubman was very wealthy. He owned three plantations in the Augusta area as well as being on the board of a bank.

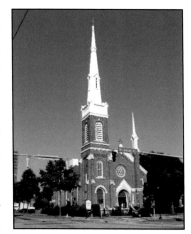

Emily's mother in Kentucky was too far away so she asked

Mr. Ware if she could marry. He said yes. So Emily Thomas, 24, of Kentucky and Richard Tubman, 52, were married. Emily had money and Richard Tubman had even more money. They were a very wealthy family. That spring, Emily took her husband Richard to meet her family. Things went well and Richard was introduced.

During her life, every summer, Emily would go to Kentucky and every winter she would come back to Augusta. Richard and Emily never had children of their own. They lived in a beautiful home on Broad Street where the Augusta Chronicle building stands today. Richard Tubman died in the arms of his wife in 1836. They had been married 18 years and he was 70 years old when he died.

At 44, Emily Tubman found herself a widow. Emily was a great entrepreneur. During the next year she tripled her net worth. Richard Tubman had put in his will that he wanted his slaves released. Emily talked to the state of Georgia and they said she could not release the slaves in Georgia. So Emily contacted the Maryland Colonization Chapter.

They had just started the country of Liberia, West Africa for released slaves. In 1844, Emily talked to her 140 slaves. She said she would be willing to pay their fare if they wanted to go to freedom in Liberia. Half of them said yes, but the other half said no. The half who said no were willing to stay in Augusta and remain her slaves. The slaves that left took her last name in thanks for their freedom. That's why, some three generations later the President of Liberia's name was William S. Tubman. He was from a family of one of Emily's released slaves.

It is estimated that Emily gave $25,000.00 a year to charities. She founded Tubman school for girls, now Tubman Middle School co-ed. She also paid for the building of "The First Christian Church" shown above. The magnolia tree to the right of the church was planted by Emily Tubman in 1872. She was a major investor in the King Mill, and she owned stock in the railroad company.

Research resources:

1. *The Story of Augusta. Cashin, Edward J. Spartanburg, SC. The Reprint Company Publishing. (1996)*
2. *Augusta, A Pictorial History. Callahan, Helen. Richmond County Historical Society Publisher. (1980)*
3. *Confederate City, Augusta Georgia 1860-1865. Corley, Florence Fleming. (1995)*
4. *Memorial History of Augusta, Georgia. Jones, Charles C. Spartanburg, SC. The Reprint Publishers. (1890)*
5. *The Brightest Arm of the Savannah, the Augusta Canal. Cashin, Edward J. (2002)*
6. *Articles from the Augusta Chronicle.*

AUGUSTA CEMETERIES

The land for the Summerville Cemetery, at John's Road and Cumming

Road, was donated by Thomas Cummings in 1824, approximately 1 ½ acres. Today the cemetery is approximately five acres, surrounded by a 5 foot high, ivy covered, brick wall with heavy wrought iron gates. The Summerville Cemetery is the final resting place of three former governors of Georgia, George W. Crawford, Charles J. Jenkins, and John Milledge. You'll also find the graves of Joseph R. Lamar and Artemis Gould.

The Walker Family Cemetery, on the campus of Georgia Regents University, is a family cemetery. When Freemen Walker sold 70 acres to the government for the Arsenal, he kept one acre for the

family cemetery. It is still an active Walker Family burial location. General W. H. T. Walker, killed in the Battle of Atlanta in 1864, is buried here as is Octavia Walker Walton LeVert. She was living in Mobile, Alabama when her aunt became seriously ill. Octavia came back to Augusta to be near her, but Octavia died before her aunt. Edgar Allen Poe's poem, *Octavia*, is written about her.

Cedar Grove Cemetery is rich in black history. In 1820 Augusta allocated 40 acres of land for the burial of slaves. They were laid to rest in wooden boxes or simply wrapped in cloth and buried in unmarked shallow graves. No index was available until after 1930. The oldest marked grave is that of Mary Jane Kent dated 1835. Some of the more

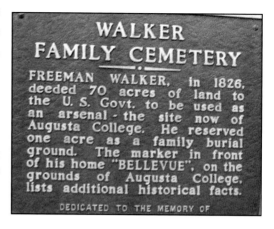

notable people buried here are Mr. James Carter Sr., Augusta's first black dentist; Dr. T.W. Josey (a high school is named for him), a physician; and Mrs. Amanda America Dickson Toomer, the richest black woman in the southeast.

The old city cemetery, Magnolia, is at the end of Walton Way. It was named for the many Magnolia trees that are in and around the cemetery. Land for the cemetery was given in 1818 by Nicholas Delaigle who owned a brick yard. In fact, you can find some of the old bricks in the walkways at Magnolia. Nicholas Delaigle is also buried there. There are 5 different Jewish sections and a Confederate section where approximately 337 soldiers and 7 generals are buried. You can also find some Union soldiers who were prisoners of war and died in Augusta.

The oldest cemetery in downtown Augusta is at Saint Paul's Episcopal Church. The cemetery was used from 1750 until about 1820. The overwhelming majority of those buried here are merchants but there are others like Robert Forsyth, the first U.S. Marshal killed in the line of duty and William Few, one of the two Georgia signers of the U.S. Constitution. Many folks with different religious backgrounds are here including several Presbyterians like the first minister, Rev. Washington McKnight.

Many churches in the Augusta area have cemeteries, including Springfield Baptist Church where 6 of their former pastors are buried in the front yard.

This highlights only a few of the local cemeteries but there are many more in North Augusta and Beech Island, South Carolina. Take some time to go to a cemetery and look at the design on the headstones. As you read them you will most likely find them to be interesting and informative. Just think, there's a story behind every gravestone - people who lived their lives, long or short. The history of Augusta can be found in her cemeteries.

Research resources:

1. *The Story of Augusta. Cashin, Edward J. Spartanburg, S. The Reprint Company Publishing. (1996)*
2. *Augusta, A Pictorial History. Callahan, Helen. Richmond County Historical Society Publisher. (1980)*
3. *Memorial History of Augusta, Georgia. Jones, Charles C. Spartanburg, SC. The Reprint Publishers. (1890)*
4. *From City to Countryside. Haltermann, Bryan M. (1997)*
5. *Haunted Augusta and Local Legends. The Augusta Chronicle. (2002)*

THE AUGUSTA ARSENAL

The Augusta Arsenal moved up from the river to the hill in 1826. The

architecture and building plans were duplicated on the Hill. One of the Arsenals most well-known soldiers was Lieutenant William T. Sherman who spent six months here in 1844. At the start of the Civil War in 1861 the Arsenal was surrendered to the Confederates and George Washington Rains took control of the Arsenal and the Gunpowder Mill by the river. The Arsenal made and repaired weapons for the Confederates and was also a hospital toward the end of the war. In May of 1865, the Arsenal was returned to the Union. During World War I the Arsenal became a center for the repair of small arms and rifles. After 1918 only a small force was stationed at the Arsenal. During that time the "Works Progress Administration," WPA, did a lot of work paving the roads and repairing the buildings.

The II World War saw a lot of growth at the Arsenal but in May of 1941 the Arsenal was closed to the public.

The Arsenal had a work force of 1800 people, 600 of whom were women. The most important function was the manufacturing of bomb sights and other lens instruments, such as telescopes and periscopes for submarines. The Arsenal also housed German prisoners of war who were used as farm laborers and to do road work. After the war in the 1950s, the government closed the Arsenal once again and the Richmond County

Board of Education received the property. There is a free museum at the corner of Katherine Street and Walton Way in the old guard house of the Augusta Arsenal.

President George Washington came to visit Augusta in May of 1791. While he was here he told George Walton and others that we should consider building an arsenal on the river. In 1816 they started building the arsenal where the mills are today. President James Monroe visited Augusta on May 16, 1819 to see the new  arsenal. 34 men were stationed there. At that time there was no canal, it was built in 1845 and the Arsenal was outside of Augusta proper.

In 1820, one of the young soldiers had just gotten married and was on leave for his honeymoon. The Arsenal Commandant, Matthew M. Payne, was visiting the Freemen Walker family at their Bellevue estate up on the hill. A fever epidemic swept through killing everyone in the Arsenal. Although Payne contacted the fever he recovered giving credit to the healthier location of Bellevue, up on the hill. He recommended that the Arsenal be moved. Freemen Walker decided he would be willing to sell 70 acres, of his 71 acre estate. The one acre he would not sell was the family cemetery. It wasn't until 1826 that Congress authorized the purchase. The Arsenal relocated in 1826 and 1827. They took some of the buildings apart down by the river, put them on wagons and hauled them to where they are today. It's interesting to note that they drove over a new road called the plank road. It would later be called Walton Way. It was called the "plank road" because at the foot of the hill it had been swampy, so they had to lay the planks to make it passable.

If you go to Georgia Regents University you'll see many of the old Arsenal buildings, plus Freemen Walker's house, Bellevue.

Research resources:

1. *The Story of Augusta. Cashin, Edward J. Spartanburg, SC. The Reprint Company Publishing. (1996)*
2. *Augusta, A Pictorial History. Callahan, Helen. Richmond County Historical Society Publisher. (1980)*
3. *Confederate City, Augusta Georgia 1860-1865. Corley, Florence Fleming. (1995)*
4. *Memorial History of Augusta, Georgia. Jones, Charles C. Spartanburg, SC. The Reprint Publishers. (1890)*
5. *The Brightest Arm of the Savannah, The Augusta Canal 1845-2000. Cashin, Edward J. (2002)*

AUGUSTA RAILROAD

Augusta has played a role in American trains from the beginning. In 1833 the first train ran from Charleston to Hamburg, South Carolina. Hamburg was just across the river from Augusta. Henry Schultz had named

Hamburg for his hometown in Germany. Augusta wouldn't let them build a railroad bridge across the Savannah River until 1837 when they were told that they would be bypassed, causing the city to reconsider.

There is an interesting story about the railroad bridge by St. Paul's Episcopal Church. Prior to the Clarks Hill Dam being built in 1954 Augusta experienced major flooding. In 1929 the river was swollen carrying uprooted trees and other debris at 36 times its normal rate. Trees could be heard crashing into the columns holding up the railroad bridge. The bridge was in major

jeopardy until someone came up with an idea. The train cars were loaded with dirt and the rain created mud, which was very heavy. The train was then pulled onto the bridge. The weight of the train made the bridge so heavy that the trees crashing into the columns didn't destroy the bridge.

Mrs. Emily Tubman, the great entrepreneur, owned stock in several railroad companies. During the Civil War Mrs. Tubman told the Confederate soldiers they could ride the train for free. Over 100,000 soldiers did just that, taking advantage of her generosity. However, "Yankees" were not so lucky and had to pay. The railroad brought many wounded soldiers to Augusta. All of the churches on Telfair Street were used as hospitals.

If you lived in Augusta before 1973 you remember Union Station which was located where the Post Office building is today. It was a big building. The only thing left from the old station sits in front of Richmond Academy on Telfair Street. It is at the top of the tower and looks like a gazebo. The last train pulled out of Union Station in the early 1970s.

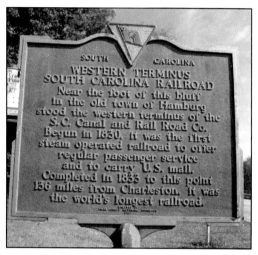

Union Station was a busy hub for five railroad companies, which is how the station got its name. It was a very busy place with cargo being shipped here and there, people catching the train to see loved ones, traveling to school or for business. President Woodrow Wilson remembered the trains arriving with Yankee prisoners and many wounded soldiers, taking some to the church his dad pastored, First Presbyterian.

The Augusta History Museum houses an old steam engine that was built in Ohio back in 1915 for the Georgia Railroad Co. That very locomotive made the run between Augusta and Atlanta, using lots of coal and water. It held 15 tons of coal and 10,800 gallons of water. The train trip to Atlanta made four stops and took 10 hours.

Research resources:

1. *The Story of Augusta. Cashin, Edward J. Spartanburg, SC. The Reprint Company Publishing. (1996)*
2. *Augusta, A Pictorial History. Callahan, Helen. Richmond County Historical Society Publisher. (1980)*
3. *Memorial History of Augusta, Georgia. Jones, Charles C. Spartanburg, SC. The Reprint Publishers. (1890)*
4. *The Brightest Arm of the Savannah, the Augusta Canal. Cashin, Edward J. (2002)*

THE HAUNTED PILLAR

Every city seems to have a "haunted" side and Augusta is no exception. The Haunted Pillar is located at the corner of Center Street, now called Fifth Street, and Broad. It is a solitary pillar with a rich history.

The pillar was part of the Lower Market built in 1837 and was right in the middle of Broad Street. At first glance as you looked at the building it looked like it could have been a church with a big bell tower and pillars on each side of the porch. But it was billed as the Lower Market or what we call today a farmer's market. Fresh produce like peaches, corn, black eyed peas and every once in a while an animal were sold at the market. There's been a lot of talk here in Augusta about slaves being sold there and some even say you can still see the bloody hand prints on the pillar. The truth is very few slaves were sold there. If a slave owner were to die they might auction his slaves there, but that didn't happen very often. It was mostly just a farmers market.

You may be wondering how a curse could be attached to an area so visible and important to the community. Accounts going back as far as 1878 talk about it, and it might still be true. In late 1877 or early 1878 a visiting preacher was holding meetings in Augusta. One day he happened to be downtown at the Lower Market. He started talking to people inside and handing out tracts. The management quickly came up to him, pulled him aside and told him he could not do that in the market. The preacher replied that he was being polite and was only interested in the spiritual well-being of the people. Again he was told he could not do it in the Lower Market. By this time the preacher was getting a little irritated. He said, "Let me tell you something, if this business finds itself torn apart and destroyed, you remember how you wouldn't let a preacher talk to the people here." A few weeks later, on the night of February 7, 1878, Augusta had a rare cyclone. It hit the Lower Market and demolished the building, leaving nothing standing except one 10 foot tall pillar. Folks remembered what the preacher had said and the word spread quickly, "Don't move the pillar or you'll die!"

Since 1878, there have been several cases of people dying. One was a man who was determined to use his bulldozer to knock down the pillar. While he was loading the bulldozer on his trailer, he got too close to the edge. The bulldozer came off the trailer, rolled over and crushed the man. He died instantly. In another case a gentleman in a pickup truck picked up a chain from his house and was heading downtown to pull the pillar down. He was involved in a vehicle accident and also died. Now the Augusta City Fathers aren't sure if this curse is true or not, but they're not going to find out. That's why the Haunted Pillar has not been moved and is still standing at the corner of Fifth and Broad Street.

Research resources:

1. *The Story of Augusta. Cashin, Edward J. Spartanburg, SC. The Reprint Company Publishing. (1996)*
2. *Augusta, A Pictorial History. Callahan, Helen. Richmond County Historical Society Publisher. (1980)*
3. *From City to Countryside. Haltermann, Bryan M. (1997)*
4. *Haunted Augusta and Local Legends. Joiner, Sean. (2002)*
5. *The Place We Call Home, A Collection of Articles About Local History. The Augusta Chronicle.*

NICHOLAS DELAIGLE

It's interesting what brings people to Augusta. Some people were born

here like Amy Grant, Hulk Hogan and Brenda Lee, just to name a few. But most people were born somewhere else and moved here. The potato famine of 1844 brought a lot of Irishmen to Augusta. Greeks, Asians and of course, a large number of Englishmen also immigrated to Georgia.

In the 1790s, during the French Revolution, a certain Frenchman came to Augusta. He was captured in France during the revolt and was sentenced to die for his part in the fighting. He was sentenced to a beheading by the guillotine and was imprisoned awaiting his death. His name was Nicholas Delaigle. If he had been beheaded the story would have ended, but Nicholas was able to escape prison and leave the country of France. He caught a ship bound for the Caribbean. Upon arriving in

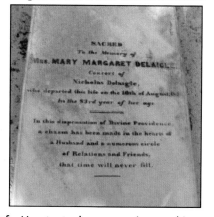

the islands he breathed a sigh of relief. He started over again, working. It wasn't long until he found himself in trouble again, life threatening trouble. Once again he took off. This time he went down to the wharf and snuck aboard a ship that was heading to the new colonies of America. Lucky for Nicholas the ship set sail, but unlucky for him he was found and was then made to work with the crew. Nicholas Delaigle thought back to the close call he had in France and how he was out of Barbados and was still alive. It was almost too much to believe. He couldn't help but wonder what the new country would hold for him. Nicholas Delaigle's life had been spared again. This time stowed away on a ship bound for the new country of America. Nicholas met a man on the ship who was traveling with his wife and they became close friends.

One day a ship was sighted. As it came closer its flag was unfurled revealing a pirate ship. The pirates quickly took control of the ship Nicholas was on and had all the men gather on deck. The Pirates then went through the ship taking anything of value. After they finished plundering the ship it was time for a little merriment. They decided to have the men of the captured ship walk the gang plank. One by one the men walked the plank and fell into the ocean where they drowned. Nicholas was handling a Masonic medallion. One of the Pirates noticed the medallion and had Nicholas step out of line. He didn't have to walk the gang plank. His close friend however did. The Pirates left the ship and went back to their own ship. After receiving help from a passing ship they proceeded on to America. This was the third time his life had been spared. When the ship docked, Nicholas along with his friend's wife, Mary Margaret, came to Augusta. They later married and had several children. Nicolas Delaigle was not a poor man. His jacket buttons were actually gold pieces that had been covered with cloth. He bought land and started a brickyard in Augusta and eventually gave the land to the city of Augusta for Magnolia Cemetery where he is now buried along with his family.

Research resources:

1. *The Story of Augusta. Cashin, Edward J. Spartanburg, SC. The Reprint Company Publishing. (1996)*
2. *Memorial History of Augusta, Georgia. Jones, Charles C. Spartanburg, SC. The Reprint Publishers. (1890)*

THE AUGUSTA CANAL

The Augusta Canal is an important part of Augusta's history going back to the year 1844. There had been talk of a canal since the early 1840s. A group of prominent and wealthy citizens had looked at the canal in Lowell, Massachusetts. Many Augustans came to support the canal project which was submitted by Colonel Henry H. Cummings. Later Cummings would to be called the father of the Augusta Canal. Because no one individual had sufficient capital to underwrite such a project, a group of men, led by former U.S. Senator John P. King, made the canal a reality. They incorporated a canal company and raised $500,000. Not everyone in Augusta was in favor of the canal. Their thoughts were that manufacturing was a "northern thing." The South raised cotton and should not be manufacturers as well. In spite of the  objections, construction began in late 1844, continuing until 1846. From the head gates located north of Augusta in Columbia County to Augusta the canal was seven miles long. The canal was for industrial use which raised the question as to where it should empty. The first plan was to be just south of town. Some protested fearing it would drop the river level in town, hurting the city. They eventually decided to go back to the river through Hawks Gully.

On November 23, 1846 water was first released into the Augusta Canal, completing the first level. The second and third levels of the canal were completed in 1848 bringing the full length of the canal to nine miles. In 1849 ownership of the canal was transferred to the city of Augusta. During the Civil War the canal played a large part in the thinking of George Washington Rains in building the Confederate Powder Mill which produced around three million pounds of gunpowder.

After the Civil War the city decided to enlarge the canal at the cost of $173,000. Green and Company were contracted and brought in over 200 men and women from China as laborers in May of 1872. After the enlargement was completed in 1875, it left the canal much as it is today. The canal is nine miles long, 11 feet deep, 106 feet wide at the bottom and 150 feet wide at the surface. Instead of the original 600 horsepower, it is now capable of producing 14,000 horsepower. The enlarged canal is outdone only by the Suez Canal.

With the enlarged canal Mayor Estes was reelected mayor. He won with a vote of two to one over Lewis D. Ford. With increased power from the canal industry started building. The Sibley Mill was built in 1880 and the J P King Mill in 1883. In April 2003 the "Augusta Canal Interpretive Center," in the Enterprise Mill, opened its doors. In October 2003, a replica of the old Petersburg boat began giving boat rides on the canal.

This is the only canal in America still doing what it was originally built to do, provide power for the mills.

Research sources:

1. *The Story of Augusta. Cashin, Edward J. Spartanburg, SC. The Reprint Company Publishing. (1996)*
2. *Augusta, A Pictorial History. Callahan, Helen. Richmond County Historical Society Publisher. (1980)*
3. *Confederate City, Augusta Georgia 1860-1865. Corley, Florence Fleming. (1995)*
4. *Memorial History of Augusta, Georgia. Jones, Charles C. Spartanburg, SC. The Reprint Publishers. (1890)*
5. *From City to Countryside. Haltermann, Bryan M. (1997)*
6. *The Brightest Arm of the Savannah, The Augusta Canal 1845-2000. Cashin, Edward J. (2002)*
7. *From City to Countryside. Haltermann, Bryan M. (1997)*

GRANDISON HARRIS – *"RESURRECTION MAN"*

Grandison Harris was a black man born in the year of 1816 in West Africa. In 1852, a 36 year old Grandison found himself on the slave

auction block in Charleston, South Carolina. That day the dean of the Medical College in Augusta came to Charleston to bid on a slave. He saw Grandison Harris and won the bid for $700. Grandison was taken to Augusta, Georgia, leaving his pregnant wife in Charleston.

It was against the law to teach slaves how to read or write, but the doctors at the Medical College taught Grandison how to read and write because they knew it would be an important part of his job. The Medical College was in need of cadavers, dead bodies, for

medical students to use for dissections. In the past they had offered 75¢ per body, but few people had taken them up on the offer. This became the job of Grandison Harris. He would read the obituaries in newspaper and find out where and when burials were planned. The main cemetery for black folks was Cedar Grove Cemetery. Late at night he would take his cart, sack(s) and a shovel and quietly go into the cemetery and find the grave. He would look and remember how everything was on the grave and then dig down to the body. If the body was in a casket Grandison would break into one end of the casket and with a firm grip and strong-arms he would pull the body out. He would then put the body into a bag and load it on his cart. Everything would then be put back on the grave in its original position. People could not tell the grave had been disturbed. The cart would then be rolled back to the Medical College on Telfair Street. The bodies would be dissected and used to teach students about the anatomy of the human body.

The faculty and the students knew about the work of Grandison Harris. Around the school he became known as the "Resurrection Man." Grave robbing was, of course, illegal but the crime was ignored and the Medical  School's faculty was never reprimanded.

When the Civil War ended, slavery ended. Harris' wife and George moved from Charleston to live with him in Augusta. Grandison left the school at the end of the civil war but returned later and became a porter for eight dollars a month.

Just think, in 1852 on the slave auction block Harris didn't know what he was going to be doing. Would he be working on a plantation as a horseman or in his master's house? But as fate would have it, he went to work for a Medical College. In the college Harris sat in on anatomy classes. In 1889 as word spread throughout the black community about the use of their dead from Cedar Grove Cemetery for dissections authorities faced civil disobedience. The school almost had its own riot. There is no record of what eventually calmed the storm in the black community.

In 1908 an enfeebled Harris made his last appearance at the school. Grandison Harris died of heart failure at the age of 95 in 1911. Three days

later, he was laid to rest in the cemetery that knew him well, Cedar Grove Cemetery. For the next 100 years people would mention the "Resurrection Man." Most people thought of it as an old wives tale. In 1989, the old Medical College building which was built in 1835, got a "face lift." The construction workers were tearing up the floor in the old kitchen and found a bone, a human bone. In a few minutes they found another bone. By the time they got the floor up they discovered there were hundreds of human bones. The authorities said between 350 to 450 people were buried there. Some of

the bones had specimen numbers written on them; a large wooden vat holding dozens of bones was also found. Workers found another vat that held body parts preserved in whiskey.

The Medical College knew the bones were from the work of Grandison Harris. When the students dissected the bodies they were buried in the Medical College building and lime was used to cut down the odor. All of the bones were put in a large crate and given to the city.

In 1998 the crate of bones was laid to rest in Cedar Grove Cemetery and a monument was erected recognizing Grandison Harris and his work.

Research resources:

The Place We Call Home, A Collection of Articles About Local History From; The Augusta Chronicle; 1997

THE SIGNERS MONUMENT

The Signers Monument in Augusta is marked by a 50 foot tall pillar in front of the Municipal building, dedicated on July 4, 1848. Two of the three Georgia signers of the "Declaration of Independence" are buried here. George Walton was the youngest signer at 26 years of age. Interestingly, not one of the Georgia signers was born in Georgia.

George Walton came to Georgia from Farmville, Virginia where he was born in 1749. He took up law in Savannah and became a Colonel in the Georgia Militia. He was injured and captured during the siege of Savannah in 1778 and traded for another high ranking officer. He became the Governor of Georgia twice. George Walton was appointed a judgeship on the Georgia Supreme Court and was also chosen Chief Justice for the state. He served six times in Congress and finished out someone else's term in the senate. He was a founding trustee of Franklin College which became the University of Georgia. He moved to Augusta in 1790 and died in 1804.

Lyman Hall was born in Wallingford, Connecticut on April 20, 1724. He was a physician who first moved to South Carolina and then to Georgia. He also signed the "Declaration of Independence." In 1781 he returned to Georgia only to head north when the British invaded. Lyman Hall's, "Knoll Plantation" was burned to the ground. He was elected Governor and served until 1784. Hall died in Burke County in 1790.

The third signer from Georgia was Button Gwinnett. Gwinnett was born in England about 1735 and immigrated to Savannah as a merchant. In

1765 he bought St. Catherine's Island, purchased slaves and tried his hand as a planter. Gwinnett was a cantankerous man and lost St. Catherine's Island and many of his possessions to creditors. He became a somewhat successful politician. In 1777, he served two months as acting Governor of Georgia but lost in the following election. A long standing feud with brothers Lachlan and George McIntosh erupted when Gwinnett was elected governor. George was the only member of the Assembly to vote against him. When Gwinnett heard that Lachlan Macintosh had been calling him a rascal and other distasteful names, he did what was common in that day and challenged Lachlan McIntosh to a duel. On May 16, 1777 the two fought a duel near Savannah. Button Gwinnett was shot. Though he did not die that day, gangrene set in around the wound and Gwinnett died three days later. Friends of McIntosh wanted the body. Though we don't know why, the friends of Gwinnett took his body and buried him secretly. Even the folks in Savannah don't know where Button Gwinnett is buried.

Research sources:

1. *The Story of Augusta. Cashin, Edward J. Spartanburg, SC. The Reprint Company Publishing. (1996)*
2. *Augusta, A Pictorial History. Callahan, Helen. Richmond County Historical Society Publisher. (1980)*
3. *Confederate City, Augusta Georgia 1860-1865. Corley, Florence Fleming. (1995)*
4. *From City to Countryside. Haltermann, Bryan M. (1997)*

JAMES HENRY HAMMOND

James Henry Hammond was born on November 15, 1807.   The descendants of the Hammond family settled in Massachusetts back in

1634. In 1802 a representative of the Hammond family came to Charleston, South Carolina. His name was Elisha Hammond.   When he landed Elisha was "sick, and a stranger to everybody," with "few clothes and but one single quarter of a dollar" in his pocket. He was a graduate of Dartmouth College and became a teacher at the Methodist Academy of Mount Bethel near Newberry, South Carolina. Several years before Elisha's father had tried to get him to go to college and become a Methodist preacher. Elisha had his own ideas believing that becoming an attorney would hold more potential for wealth.

Elisha married Catherine Fox Spann, from Columbia, in 1806. Elisha and Catherine had their first child on November 15, 1807, at Stony Battery near Newberry and named him James Henry Hammond. Three more children followed, Caroline Augusta, Marcus Claudius Marcellus and John Fox. At 16 years old James Henry had already been prepared for college by his father; he entered the junior class at South Carolina College, graduating fourth in a class of 33 in December of 1825. In 1828, at the age of 21 Hammond became a lawyer achieving his father's ambition.

Elisha moved to Macon, Georgia in 1828 to head its local Academy. He died suddenly on July 9, 1829, apparently of yellow fever.

In 1830, James Henry Hammond met Catherine Elizabeth Fitzsimons, a 16-year-old Charleston heiress. She was from a wealthy family. Her father had died five years prior to their meeting. James proposed to Catherine in 1831 marriage but her family objected on the grounds that

Catherine was too young and that Hammond was obviously a fortune hunter. Catherine's family asked Hammond to renounce her dower. Outraged, he refused to do so, and continued to press his suit ardently with Catherine who in turn pressured her family to allow her to marry him. Her mother eventually consented and they married in June of 1831. Hammond claimed that "a finer, more high-minded and devoted woman never lived." Catherine was only 17 years old and James Henry 24 years old. Through the marriage James Henry received a plantation of about 7500 acres in Barnwell District at Silver Bluff on the Savannah River, 147 slaves, and much farm equipment. He also gained connections with the prominent Hampton family through Catherine's older sister Ann who was the wife of Wade Hampton II.

After the wedding, James Henry and Catherine moved to Silver Bluff Plantation. James Henry became a planter and Catherine gave him five sons over the next five years: James Henry (always known as Harry), Christopher Fitzsimmons, Edward Spann, William Cashel, and Charles Julius.

James Henry had a different outlook on women, believing a woman's job was to have children and raise them. It is thought that even though he said some nice things to say about Catherine, he probably never loved her. His actions and his view on marriage and women make it doubtful that he had any feelings for her or that he even could develop a loving relationship with a female.

James Henry was successful in cultivating several thousand acres. "Hammond claimed that when he married Catherine, her property had been so badly managed that it had produced an annual income of only $600, and that he had increased it to 21,000 dollars."

Despite his move from Columbia to Silver Bluff Plantation his political interests continued, running for Congress, and winning. Before the close of the first session of Congress, Hammond's ulcerous stomach, which he complained of throughout his adult life, began to trouble him. He blamed it on life in Washington and resigned. Physicians advised him to travel so he decided upon an extended trip abroad. Late in July of 1836 James Henry, Catherine and their 4 year-old son, Harry, sailed for Europe. Most of their time was spent in England, France, and Italy. Their travels afforded them the opportunity to purchase many pieces of art, sculptures, as well as paintings. They returned to Silver Bluff in August of 1837.

James Henry threw himself into the process of making the plantation profitable. He soon grew impatient with the thin Barnwell land and the low cotton prices of 1837. In the spring of 1838 he took a month's journey on horseback through Georgia and Florida in search of cheap and fertile land. What he found was that "good land was high and cheap land poor." He rode back to Silver Bluff and began to drain and ditch in an effort to improve what he already had. James Henry Hammond scored his success when low prices compelled planters to increase production to make a profit. Having married Catherine for her wealth he proceeded to exploit her property to the fullest, hauling enormous amounts of mock up from the Savannah River to enrich the land he was cultivating. Hammond shipped his cotton through Augusta to his factory in Savannah. He never used the new Charleston Hamburg Railroad, which started in 1833.

In 1839 he let his friends in the state legislature know that he was available to run for governor of South Carolina. Expecting to win the election Hammond built a fine townhouse in Columbia, but he did not win. James Henry Hammond returned to his plantation house, "Silverton" at Silver Bluff.

In December of 1842 James Henry Hammond was elected governor of South Carolina defeating R.F.W. Allston in a close vote of 83 to 76. During his time as governor James Henry Hammond contributed two big things. He reorganized the state militia and he oversaw the establishment of the Citadel in Charleston as the state's military Academy.

In 1846 Hammond's political career came to an abrupt halt. His friends had brought his name before the Legislature as a candidate for the United States Senate. His candidacy was blocked by opposition of his wife's brother-in-law, Wade Hampton II, who was also the father of four daughters. Ann, his wife was dead, but his daughters as teenagers were frequent visitors to their Aunt Catherine's house. It was well documented that James Henry had a roving eye and the girls apparently did not object to frolicking with their uncle, the governor, but the frolics soon went beyond the innocent. Hammond later wrote of all four "simultaneously covering him with kisses while he enjoyed with them every intimacy but the ultimate." After two years the oldest niece, outraged by something James Henry had done, ran to her aunt and the tale was out. In 1844 Hammond left Columbia following his term as governor.

Finally, in 1846, when James Henry was being considered for the Senate, Wade Hampton, who kept the matter a private family affair until this time, stopped Hammond's candidacy with the threat of unleashing the scandal. Catherine Hammond did stand by her man the whole time. In 1849 Catherine presented James Henry with a daughter, Elizabeth, their eighth and last child. However, in December of 1850 Catherine left James Henry because of his affair with his slave, Louisa. Mrs. Hammond had told John Henry to give up his slave but he wouldn't. She packed up the kids and went to stay with her parents in Augusta, in the Hill area. A year and a half later Mrs. Hammond and the children still had not returned home. The blame of course was not his, "I trace it all to the horrible connection, which Satan seduced me into forming with the vulgar Fitzsimmons family, whose low Irish descent and hypocrisy can only be compared with their low-Irish pride, selfishness and utter want of refinement and tone."

In 1852 Catherine Hammond and the children had not returned. John Henry's slave, Louisa, was out of the house. Louisa was given to Mrs. Fitzsimmons as her personal maid. Louisa arrived at the Fitzsimmons house in Charleston, November of 1852. Catherine had been gone a little over two years.

In the spring of 1855, James Henry Hammond found what he wanted and purchased a house and 400 acres of land at Beech Island, a community in Edgefield district on the

South Carolina bank of the Savannah River. The house faced west toward Augusta, 7 miles away and stood on ground close to the edge of a bank of reddish clay and sand that sloped sharply away in front of it, thus the name "Redcliffe." About a quarter of a mile east of the house, Hammond selected the site upon which he would build a larger and more imposing home in keeping with his social position.

In May of 1857 Senator Andrew Pickens Butler died. Hammond told Simms that he did not want the office, for South Carolina had "committed a great and wanton outrage upon me." But Hammond was the most acceptable candidate. On the third ballot the

legislator elected him to the Senate and he accepted. The "outsider" once in the Senate, made a speech on March 4, 1858 for which he is still remembered. It contained John Henry's thesis about the "mudsills of society" and the phrase "cotton is king." He defended slavery by observing that all civilizations had a class of servants to do the menial duties. The North had its working class, the South its slaves; these workers who performed the drudgery of life, provided the foundations or mudsills, upon which great societies developed. And there could be no civil war, for "you dare not make war on cotton. No power on earth dares to make war upon it, Cotton is king." Hammond never wavered in his support of slavery. He expressed his views in speeches.

He had two banquets in his honor held after the adjournment of Congress in 1858. The first was on July 22 at Beech Island. He received only passing notice. But the second speech given on October 29, 1858 at Barnwell Courthouse received national coverage and was very well received in northern newspapers.

With the election of Abraham Lincoln in November 1860 Hammond resigned from the Senate.

In December 1860 South Carolina seceded from the union and Hammond returned to Redcliffe Plantation. The house when completed in 1859 came to designate the new residents as well as the land. When the war came in April of 1861 Hammond gave the Confederacy his full financial support. By 1860 half of his estate consisted of Confederate bonds. Deeply troubled by the fall of Atlanta on September 1, 1864 and expecting Sherman to march across Georgia to the sea, Hammond willed himself to die. "This war," he then said, "will terminate suddenly within six months. I do not care to look behind the veil enough that everything I have worked for, the labors of my life will all be upset." On the day before his death, while lying on a couch in the library at Redcliffe, he called Stan to his side and told him that he wished to be buried in the woods on the highest ground where there would be a view of Augusta and the Sand Hills, "but mind . . . if we are subjected, run a plow over my grave."

James Henry Hammond died on November 13, 1864, two days before his 57th birthday.

Research sources:

1. *The Hammonds of Radcliffe; by Bleser, Carol; Copyright 1981; Published by Oxford University Press.*
2. *James Henry Hammond and the Old South, A Design for Mastery; by Drew Gilpin Faust; copyright 1985; LSU Press.*

THE CONFEDERATE GUN POWDER WORKS

For over 140 years the towering brick obelisk called the "Confederate Powder Works" chimney has stood proudly in Augusta. It is located on Goodrich Street right in front of the Sibley Mill.

On July 10, 1861 Confederate President, Jefferson Davis, selected Colonel George Washington Rains to find a site and build a gunpowder mill. At that time Jefferson Davis knew that war was eminent with the North. The South had no factories making gunpowder except a small stamping mill

in the interior of Tennessee. A rapid tour of the south was taken to find a suitable location. In his own words Colonel Rains said Augusta was chosen for several reasons, "for its central position, for its canal transportation and water power, its railroad facilities, and especially for the security from attack." He sent men to see how gunpowder was made and then had them come back to Augusta. He ordered saltpeter and other ingredients that gunpowder used and began building. One building would be too dangerous so Colonel Rains hired William Pendleton, formally of the large Tredegar Iron works in Richmond, Virginia, Miller Grant a civil engineer from Savannah and C. Shaler Smith, an Augusta architect. In all 26 buildings were built using 5 million bricks. The powder mill was on a track of 140 acres that extended nearly two miles along the banks of the canal.

On July 10, 1861 Confederate President, Jefferson Davis, instructed Colonel George Washington Rains to build a gunpowder factory. He was given carte-blanche to money, with instructions to just do it, ASAP. The work began. Twenty-six buildings were built, supplies were shipped in and gunpowder was made. The first gunpowder was made on April 13, 1862; just nine months after Colonel Rains received his orders. Even the North said the gunpowder made here was good after capturing some and using it against the South. The Power Works Mill produced some 3,000,000 pounds during the Civil War.

There has always been a question as to why General Sherman didn't come to Augusta on his march to the sea in 1864. He marched to Atlanta and fought the Battle of Atlanta. That was the battle in which General William H. T. Walker, an Augustan, lost his life. Sherman burned Atlanta to the ground. The people in Augusta expected him to come there next. The city of Augusta talked about burning their cotton bales. Fictitious telegrams were sent advising general so and so to come to Augusta and be with general so and so. None of these messages were true. But Sherman didn't come; he marched to Savannah burning everything in his path. The people of Savannah met Sherman outside of the town asking him not to burn the town. Sherman didn't burn Savannah. General Sherman sent a telegraph to President Lincoln giving him Savannah as a Christmas gift. After a short time, General Sherman marched north to Columbia and burned about a third of that city. The late historian, Dr. Edward Cashin, purposed the reason Sherman didn't burn Augusta was that he had a girlfriend who lived here. We do know that Sherman came to the Augusta Arsenal and stayed a few months, long before the Civil War. Whatever the real reason he didn't come and he didn't destroy the Gunpowder Mill.

After the war, the editor of the Augusta newspaper wrote a letter to General Sherman asking him the all-important question, "Why didn't you burn the gunpowder Mill." A few days later a letter came from General Sherman. In the letter he said he was sorry to not have burned it. He said, "If not burning it has caused confusion I can send for the guys to get together again and we can come down and finish the task." That was the last of the correspondence. After the war, on October 31, 1872 the city of Augusta bought the powder mill buildings for $32,000.00. The buildings were demolished, all but the stately obelisk that is. The chimney stands 176 feet tall and it is a memorial to the men who died during the Civil War.

Research sources:

1. *The Story of Augusta. Cashin, Edward J. Spartanburg, SC. The Reprint Company Publishing. (1996)*
2. *Augusta, A Pictorial History. Callahan, Helen. Richmond County Historical Society Publisher. (1980)*
3. *Confederate City, Augusta Georgia 1860-1865. Corley, Florence Fleming. (1995)*
4. *Memorial History of Augusta, Georgia. Jones, Charles C. Spartanburg, SC. The Reprint Publishers. (1890)*
5. *From City to Countryside. Published with the cooperation of Historic Augusta, Inc. Haltermann, Bryan M. (1997)*
6. *The Brightest Arm of the Savannah, The Augusta Canal 1845-2000. Cashin, Edward J. (2002)*

CHARLES DAWSON TILLY

Charles Dawson Tilly was born June 16, 1845 in Carlow, Ireland. "He entered Dublin University at an early age and finished his education in Paris. He then came to the United States and in 1869 was enticed to go to Augusta, Georgia by Major Branch of the firm of "Branch   Scott & Co." and whose employment he continued until 1873, when he entered into his own business. He was always noted as a businessman of energy and correctness. It is said he had an uncle who was a clergyman of the established Church of Ireland. His mother and father had been dead for several years. A sister is said to have married an English nobleman." [Facts per his obituary, 1875]

Mr. Charles Tilly had moved into the house owned by Mary Clarke de L'Aigle on Greene Street in Augusta. Mary de L'Aigle was a widow with three children who had turned her home into a boarding house to help make ends meet. Mary built the house in 1873 and Charles Tilly rented a room in the basement of the house where it stands today across from the Signers' Monument.

The year was 1875 and Charles Ratcliff lived in Augusta. Word got back to Charles Tilly that Radcliffe was accusing him of having an affair with Mary. Well, Charles Tilly did the proper thing. As a gentleman he told Radcliffe to take back his words or he would challenge him to a duel. Charles Ratcliff did not take back his words and prepared to duel with Tilly. On December 15, 1875, on Sandbar Ferry Road near the Savannah River, the duel took place. Dueling was legal at the time and over the years many duels had been fought there. On this day Charles met Charles, dueling with pistols. In the fight Tilly was mortally

 wounded. He was taken back to his room in the de L'Aigle house, where he died two days later on December 17, 1875. Mr. Tilly was buried in the family plot of the young widow whose honor he was defending in the duel.

Later the law changed in Georgia and dueling became illegal. The last legal duel was between Charles Tilly and Charles Radcliff. Mary Clarke de L'Aigle's daughter, Louise, donated money years later to build the office building of Magnolia Cemetery in honor of her mother and ordered that Mr. Tilly's portrait be hung in the rotunda where it hangs today.

Research sources:

1. *Jerry W. Murphy, Records Clerk Public Works Cemeteries Section, Augusta, Georgia*
2. *"Cemetery holds wealth of history" Augusta Chronicle April 20, 2002, Staff writer Sylvia Cooper.*

CONFEDERATE MONUMENT

The Civil War in America was fought over several reasons. One was

slavery, the right to own slaves. But the main reason was over states' rights. The United States had won its freedom from England less than a hundred years before. The South looked at the Civil War as a way for them to leave the Union and start their own country. When Abraham Lincoln was elected president in 1861 he ran on the platform that slave states would remain slave states and states that were free would remain free, but any new state coming into the Union would be a free state. When Lincoln was elected, the southern states decided they wanted their own country, "The Confederate States of America." So the war came about. President Lincoln did not want different countries in America, just different states under one government. When the South seceded it forced the Union to war. The Civil War was a deadly and bloody war, family against family and friend against friend. The Civil War lasted over four long years with hundreds of thousands of casualties.

After the surrender in April 1865 reconstruction began in the southern states. The southern population had to take an oath to one country, the United States. When Confederate President, Jefferson Davis, was captured in South Georgia, he was shackled in chains and marched through Augusta to the train station on his way north. Men would take off their hats and women cried as he walked by. The South had been defeated. The Confederate Monument in Augusta was brought to life in 1868 when the "Ladies Memorial Association" was organized to care for the graves of the Confederate dead and create a Monument to their memory.

Mrs. John Carter was president of the "Ladies Memorial Association" in 1868. Five years later the Ladies Association re-organized under the presidency of Mrs. M.E. Walton. They advertised for designs for the Monument. The model selected was done by "Van Gunden and Young" of Philadelphia. T. Markwalter of Augusta, who had a shop on Broad Street, was chosen to execute the design. The statues were carved in Italy out of Carrara marble. By the way, the statues on the Monument are life size. The Italian carver Antonio Fontana visited America and in his travels he came to Augusta and while looking at the monument recognized his work. He had worked from pictures of the men. The "Ladies Memorial Association" decided to place the Monument on Broad Street between Macintosh and Jackson Streets, that's 7th St. and 8th St. today. The cornerstone was laid on Memorial Day, April 26, 1875. General Clement Evans speech was telegraphed all over the country that day. The Monument took Markwalter three years to build at the cost of $20,934, paid for by the Association. On October 31, 1878, an estimated crowd of 10,000 people stood on Broad Street. Mrs. Thomas J. Jackson, "Stonewalls" widow, was guest of honor. Charles C. Jones of Augusta gave a great speech.

The Monument has four Confederate Generals. Robert E. Lee represents the Confederacy; Stonewall Jackson represents the State of Virginia; Thomas R. R. Cobb represents the State of Georgia; and William H. T. Walker the City of Augusta. The place of honor at the top of the monument is an anonymous enlisted soldier (the model's name was Berry Benson from North Augusta). On the monument is written, *"No nation rose so white and fair, none fell so pure of crime."*

Research sources:

1. *The Story of Augusta. Cashin, Edward J. Spartanburg, SC. The Reprint Company Publishing. (1996)*
2. *Augusta, A Pictorial History. Callahan, Helen. Richmond County Historical Society Publisher. (1980)*
3. *Memorial History of Augusta, Georgia. Jones, Charles C. Spartanburg, SC. The Reprint Publishers. (1890)*

THE COTTON MILLS

Cotton played an important role in Augusta's history. Governor James Hammond, of South Carolina said, "Cotton was King." Until 1921 Augusta was the second largest inland cotton market in the world, with Memphis being first. At its peak, 500,000 bales of cotton were going through Augusta annually. With lots of cotton and the canal for power, the mills did well. In the area where the Confederate Gunpowder Mill had been new mills sprang up. The Sibley Mill was built in 1880 and the J P. King Mill was built in 1883.

The Sibley Mill was built to look like the "Confederate Gunpowder Mill." The mill was named for one of the organizers, Josiah Sibley. The Sibley Mill received 100% of its power from the canal.

When the Enterprise Mill shut down Mr. Clay Boardman, from Augusta,

bought the building, refurbished it and now leases it to businesses like the "Augusta Metropolitan Convention and Visitors Bureau," the "Canal Interpretive Center" as well as others. The top floor of the mill has been turned into condominiums. The Enterprise Mill, although not a working mill, gets all of its power from the canal. The canal produces enough electricity to supply all the power needed for the businesses and condominiums in the Enterprise Mill.

One mill still operating in Augusta is the J.P. King Manufacturing Company. The initial investors' meeting was held to organize the new company on June 1, 1881. The major investor was Emily Thomas Tubman, investing four years before her death, in 1885. Her name is not in bright lights, however, because she was a woman in a man's world. The shareholders met again in December of 1881. During that meeting they elected former mayor, Charles Estes, as the company's first president. J. P. King Manufacturing Company began operations in October 1883. The original building was four stories tall and contained around 35,000 square feet. The walls at the front of the building are 3 feet thick and the windows have been bricked up because air-conditioning was brought into the building. Before that, you would open the windows for ventilation. The J. P. King Mill was purchased in 1968 by Spartan Mills for 10 million dollars. They had over 600,000 square feet and almost 1500 employees. About 30 years later the Spartan Mills went bankrupt. On that Friday people who had worked there for years were handed a pink slip and told not to return to work Monday. Central Textiles of Cincinnati started operating the mill at that time. Fifty percent of their electrical power comes from the canal and the rest from Georgia Power.

Research sources:

1. *The Story of Augusta. Cashin, Edward J. Spartanburg, SC. The Reprint Company Publishing. (1996)*
2. *Augusta, A Pictorial History. Callahan, Helen. Richmond County Historical Society Publisher. (1980)*
3. *Confederate City, Augusta Georgia 1860-1865. Corley, Florence Fleming. (1995)*
4. *Memorial History of Augusta, Georgia. Jones, Charles C. Spartanburg, SC. The Reprint Publishers. (1890)*
5. *From City to Countryside. Published with the cooperation of Historic Augusta, Inc. Haltermann, Bryan M. (1997)*
6. *The Brightest Arm of the Savannah, The Augusta Canal 1845-2000. Cashin, Edward J. (2002)*
7. *From City to Countryside. Haltermann, Bryan M. (1997)*

THE COTTON EXCHANGE

In 1736 the economic base in Augusta was furs, well, deer skins; only

about 5% were really furs. In 50 years, about 1785, tobacco became the cash flow crop. In 1850 cotton became the main economic base. It began in 1793 when Eli Whitney invented the cotton gin while visiting a friend on Rocky Creek, just south of Augusta. The cotton gin was able to get the seed out of the cotton which made cotton easier to work with. Many farmers switched to growing cotton with the invention of the Cotton Gin. At the height of the cotton boom Augusta was the second largest inland cotton market in the world, trailing only Memphis, Tennessee. Men from as far away as England, Germany, South America, India and France came to Augusta because of the cotton. In 1872 The Cotton Exchange was formed with

the sole purpose of buying and selling cotton. Over the next fourteen years the men knew they needed their own building. So in 1886, for $9,000, they built the Cotton Exchange Building on Reynolds Street with brick. The building is a typical high Victorian style with iron columns in the front cast at Lombard's foundry in Augusta. The building was often surrounded by such tightly packed cotton bales that it was said a child could jump from one bale to another for a mile without touching the ground. Each bale of cotton weighed 500 pounds. Between 1912 and 1920 approximately 500,000 bales of cotton went through the cotton exchange annually.

At its peak the Cotton Exchange Building on Reynolds Street had 200 members, 200 men that is; women and children were not allowed in the building. The men were required to dress in business attire. There were eight phone booths in the exchange and a weather map in the hall showing what the weather was around the country. A ticker-tape machine was also there and a 40 foot blackboard along one wall. When prices came across the wire a marker would go and mark it on the blackboard. Even John D. Rockefeller would come to the Cotton Exchange when he vacationed in Augusta.

In the city fire of 1916 the building did not burn down but it did lose its roof. In 1921 the boll weevil invaded Georgia. The boll weevil would burrow into the cotton and destroy it. The only way to kill the boll weevil was to burn the cotton field. The days of "King Cotton" had drawn to a close. The Cotton Exchange stayed open but there wasn't much business. The Exchange Building was last used by Cotton Brokers in 1964. Since 1964 the building has been used for many different purposes including a church renting it for its youth choir and the Augusta Metropolitan Convention and Visitors Bureau as a Welcome Center. In 1978, the building was entered into the National Register of Historic Places and in 1988 Mr. Bill Moore, of Aiken, SC, purchased the building. It was in great need of repair. With a grant from the City of Augusta Moore painstakingly restored the building to its original condition. During the restoration Charlie Whitney, a direct descendant of Eli Whitney, came into the building and told the workers that there used to be a blackboard on the wall behind the drywall. They started chipping the drywall off and found the blackboard with writing on it from years ago. The building cost $9,000 to build but it cost $750,000 to restore. In the year 2004, Bill Moore sold the building to "Georgia Bank and Trust Co." The blackboard is still visible in the building.

Research resources:

1. *The Story of Augusta. Cashin, Edward J. Spartanburg, SC. The Reprint Company Publishing. (1996)*
2. *Augusta, A Pictorial History. Callahan, Helen. Richmond County Historical Society Publisher. (1980)*
3. *Memorial History of Augusta, Georgia. Jones, Charles C. Spartanburg, SC. The Reprint Publishers. (1890)*
4. *From City to Countryside. Published with the cooperation of Historic Augusta, Inc. Haltermann, Bryan M. (1997)*
5. *Articles from the Augusta Chronicle.*

AMANDA AMERICA DICKSON

Augusta was once home to one of the richest black lady's in the Southeast. The Dickson family was of the wealthy planter class. They lived in Hancock County and owned more land in the county than anyone else. One day in February of 1849, David Dickson was out riding his horse checking his fields. As he rode up to one field he saw the slaves working and beside the field were slave children playing. David Dickson recognized one of the young females as belonging to his mother. With purpose he rode over to her, reached down, lifted her up and sat her on the horse behind his saddle and rode off. As her family remembered years later, "...and that was the end of that." The slave girl's name was Julia Francis. She was only 13 years old. David at the time was 40. Even though it was against the law Julia became pregnant with his child and gave birth to a daughter on November 20, 1849. Her daughter's name was Amanda America Dickson. Unlike other white fathers who having mulatto children gave them over to slavery, David Dickson did not. David claimed Amanda as his child and brought her into the big house as a member of his family. She stayed in Elizabeth Dickson's room, David's mother and Amanda's grandmother. Julia, Amanda's mother, worked in David's kitchen. Throughout her childhood David enjoyed time with his daughter. He wasn't ashamed to tell people visiting him that Amanda was his. Amanda grew up with love, money and great opportunities.

Amanda America Dickson, a mulatto child, was treated as a part of the family and learned to read and write and even learned to play the piano. After the Civil War in 1865, Amanda America married her 29 year old white cousin, Charles Eubanks. Amanda left home in 1865 moving to a new plantation to live with her husband. They had their first son, Julian

Henry, in 1866 and their second son, Charles Green, in 1870. On July 31, 1873, after only eight years of marriage, Charles Eubanks died.

Twelve years later in February of 1885 David Dickson died at the age of 76. He was buried in the garden of the Dickson family home in Hancock County. Two weeks later on March 2, 1885 David Dickson's will was read. Her father had made Amanda and her children the largest property owners in Hancock County, Georgia. The will warned that if any person contested the will, his or her legacy would be revoked. Instantly, however, 79 of David Dickson's white relatives came forward objecting to the will being admitted to probate. This started a huge court battle. The Superior Court ruled in favor of David Dickson's will in November of 1885. The Georgia Supreme Court upheld that ruling on June 13, 1887. On July 15, 1886 Amanda moved to Augusta purchasing a large brick home at 484 Telfair Street for $6,098 dollars. Amanda received in the will a little more than half a million dollars. On July 14, 1892 Amanda married Nathan Toomer of Perry, Georgia. They were only married about a year when Amanda America Dickson Toomer died on June 11, 1893. She was only 43 years old and was laid to rest wearing her wedding dress.

Amanda was one of the great historical figures of Augusta. She is buried in the Cedar Grove Cemetery.

Research resources:

Woman of Color Daughter of Privilege. Leslie, Kent Anderson. The University of Georgia Press. (1995)

WYLLY BARRON

Wylly Barron was born in the year 1806, about 25 years after the Revolutionary War. When Wylly was in his 50s he had a job at the Atkinson Hotel on Ellis Street in Augusta. His job was to manage the gambling in the hotel. While Barron was growing up he appreciated the finer things in life. He grew to be six feet tall, slender and dark. His clothing was fashionable and extreme and the sparkling gems he wore made him a flashy person you wouldn't forget. In the 1860s, while

Barron was managing the gambling at the hotel, a terrible incident happened. A young man entered the hotel and started gambling. He quickly lost all his money. He approached Wylly Barron and asked for a loan, but Mr. Barron refused his request. The man was very upset and responded, "You have taken everything I have. When you die may you not have even a grave to shelter you!" It is said that the man then went out and committed suicide. This incident caused Wylly to change the gambling rules at the Atkinson Hotel. If your position in life, like a bank teller, caused you to handle money or if your salary was not sufficient to permit gambling you would not be allowed to gamble. If the guest protested he was ejected. Minors were also barred from playing. This incident also caused Wylly Barron to give much of his money to charities.

The curse of the dead gambler haunted Wylly Barron and made him think about his future. In 1870 he had a granite tomb built in Magnolia Cemetery and made sure his last will and testament was up-to-date. In his will he asked to be buried in a steel coffin and after his death that the key to the gate and door of his grave be taken out and thrown into the Savannah River. According to cemetery records, Barron died in 1894, at

the age of 88. In the last few years of his life, Wylly Barron lost considerable property. When he died there was not enough money to buy the prescribed metal coffin. His remains were bricked over inside the vault. The keyhole was sealed and the keys thrown into the Savannah River. Today, there is no known key to either fence or vault.

Wylly Barron's epitaph reads: *"Farewell vain work, I know enough of thee, And now am careless what thou sayest of me, thy smiles I could not, nor thy frowns I fear, My cares are passed, my head lies quiet here. What faults you knew of me, take care to shun, And look at home—, enough there's to be done."*

Research sources:

1. *Jerry W. Murphy, Records Clerk Public Works Cemeteries Section, Augusta, Georgia*
2. *http://www.augustaga.gov*

SACRED HEART

Augusta is well known as a city of churches representing all denominations including Baptist, Methodist, Presbyterian, Episcopal, Disciples of Christ, Catholic, and others. Catholics were one of the first denominations to practice their faith in Augusta. In 1811 the city trustees

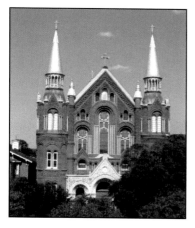

gave the property between 7th and 8th Streets and between Telfair and Walker Street for a Catholic Church building. The first building was erected in 1843. The cornerstone for "Church of the Most Holy Trinity" was laid in 1857. So many Irish immigrated during the potato famine of 1844 that they packed the building. In 1873 Bishop William Gross of the Savannah Diocese invited Father Theobald and Father Joseph Heidenkamp, two Jesuit priests, to come to Augusta and accept a new parish. The new parish boundaries had to be set up. Bishop Gross called upon the editor of the Augusta Chronicle, Patrick Walsh, to chair an advisory board. Bishop Gross acted upon the advice of Welch's committee and on March 14, 1874 "Sacred Heart Parish" was established. With money pledged by

the parishioners Father Butler was able to buy Charles Roland's house and lot on Greene Street for $10,000.

The Jesuit Priests had started back in the year of 1534 by a Spanish soldier, Ignatius of Loyola. The Society of Jesus or Jesuits are primarily

a teaching order and the Jesuit Priests would not come to Augusta unless a school was also going to be established. The school building was built first but the Diocese asked Father Butler to wait on building the new church building. Father Butler used the school building as a church until approval was given in 1898 to build the church building. Patrick Walsh presided at the meeting for "Sacred Heart Catholic Church." On August 22, 1897 Father Butler and Brother Cornelius Otten were here. Brother Otten had built "Sacred Heart

Church" in Galveston, Texas. The cornerstone was laid for the church on February 20, 1898 and the building was completed December 2, 1900 and ready to be used. The dedication was more elaborate then the Cornerstone Celebration. Cardinal Gibbons, of Baltimore, Maryland, was

there for the dedication. The church building was an architectural wonder. It was made out of 13 different brick designs which were laid on granite and limestone blocks at the base. Stepping into the building, even today, is like entering a European

cathedral. The ceilings are very high and the acoustics are outstanding. Almost half a million bricks were used in the structure and were made locally across the river in Hamburg, South Carolina. The stained-glass windows in front of the church were made in Cincinnati, Ohio and the windows on the sides and back were made in Munich, Germany. They were installed in the church before the end of 1900. In 1960 the windows had an estimated value of a quarter of a million dollars.

After the city fire of 1916 people moved away from the area and the Parish attendance declined. The Jesuits left on July 15, 1963. The Savannah Diocese kept the church open but with few people and huge repair bills they eventually had no choice but to close the building. The last Mass was celebrated on Sunday, July 4, 1971 and sadly the church was deconsecrated. The Diocese decided to combine Immaculate Conception, Sacred Heart and Most Holy Trinity churches. The Diocese tried to sell the old building asking $200,000. It was during this time that the building was listed on the National Registry of Historic Places. After 1971 homeless people broke in and started using the building and it disintegrated even more. There was talk at that time of tearing down the building and using the land for part of the expressway. On August 31, 1982 news broke that "Knox Limited" had bought the building to save it, spending huge amounts of money to repair the building. All of the stained-glass windows were removed, re-leaded and then reinstalled. The building, except the ceiling, has been repainted. Today the building is called, "The Sacred Heart Cultural Center" and is used for special occasions such as weddings, graduations and special meetings. The building is open to the public.

Research resources:

1. *The Story of Augusta. Cashin, Edward J. Spartanburg, SC. The Reprint Company Publishing. (1996)*
2. *Augusta, A Pictorial History. Callahan, Helen. Richmond County Historical Society Publisher. (1980)*
3. *Memorial History of Augusta, Georgia. Jones, Charles C. Spartanburg, SC. The Reprint Publishers. (1890)*
4. *From City to Countryside, a Guidebook to the Landmarks of Augusta, GA. Haltermann, Bryan M. (1997)*
5. *The Story of Sacred Heart. Cashin, Edward J. (1987)*

MAJOR ARCHIBALD BUTT

Archibald Butt lived in Augusta at the turn of the 20th century and never married. His story begins in 1908. Landon Thomas, who was manager of the J. P. King Mill, a nephew of Emily Tubman, invited the President elect

William Howard Taft to visit Augusta. Taft visited with his running mate,

John Sherman. They came after the election on November 19, 1908 and stayed at the Terrett Cottage on Milledge Road. Taft thoroughly enjoyed his visit and the men ended up staying in Augusta the entire winter.

He returned to Washington in March of 1909 for his Inauguration. Taft visited Augusta several times, staying at the Bon Air Hotel. President Roosevelt brought Archibald Butt to Washington as his aid. Archie, as he was called, did a good job and when Taft became president, Archibald Butt stayed on as an aid to Taft. A close friendship developed between President Taft and Major Butt. The press said he "was so close to the President, he was considered a younger brother." President Taft recognized the hard work Archie had been doing and one day President Taft offered him a vacation. Archibald Butt decided to go to Europe and found the trip very relaxing and thoroughly enjoyed his time. He was scheduled to leave from England April 10, 1912 and head home.

On April 10, 1912, Archie Butt boarded a brand-new ship on its maiden voyage from England. It was the largest ship in the world, boasting a length of four city blocks and the height of an eleven story building. With modern technology the ship was built so that it wouldn't sink. The name of the ship was the Titanic. Four days later on April 14, the Titanic was in the icy waters off the coast of Canada and the lookout yelled, "Iceberg ahead," but it was too late and the ship couldn't maneuver fast enough. It hit the iceberg, not hard but a glancing blow. The captain of the ship went below to inspect the damage and came up sometime later issuing the order to abandon ship. Passengers came on deck laughing. They all said the ship couldn't be sinking because they were on the Titanic but soon enough the awful truth began dawning on the passengers. There were 2,227 people on board the ship and they only had enough lifeboats to save 1,100 people. Pandemonium swept the ship. Men were to let women and children get into the lifeboats first. A frightened man jumped into a lifeboat. Archibald Butt reached in and pulled him out saying, "women will be attended to first or I'll break every bone in your body." Archibald placed Marie Young, from Augusta, Georgia, into the lifeboat. The last words he said to her were, "Will you kindly remember me to all the folks back home?" Her lifeboat was lowered into the water and set adrift. Looking back she could see Major Butt standing on the bridge arm-in-arm with millionaire businessman John Jacob Astor.

On April 15, 1914 President Taft came to Augusta. He dedicated the bridge on 15th Street over the canal to his friend Major Butt, buried with the Titanic at sea. The bridge has four lions on it representing the courage of Augustan, Major Archibald Butt.

Research resources:

1. *The Story of Augusta. Cashin, Edward J. Spartanburg, SC. The Reprint Company Publishing. (1996)*
2. *Augusta, A Pictorial History. Callahan, Helen. Richmond County Historical Society Publisher. (1980)*
3. *The Brightest Arm of the Savannah, The Augusta Canal. Cashin, Edward J. (2002)*

SUMMERVILLE, GEORGIA

The last of the Appalachian Mountains is called "The Hill" in Augusta. It's where the Piedmont joins the coastal plain and scientists tell us that Summerville used to be the ocean shoreline. Summerville or Sand Hills was not heavily populated in the late 1700s. During the Revolutionary War, in 1780, Elijah Clarke and his forces came up the road named Battle Row, fighting the British all the way. Some men, like George Walton, John Leach and George Walker, received large tracts of land after the Revolutionary War. In 1800 a titled Englishman, Lord Thomas Sandwich and his wife came to Augusta and started a special school on the Hill. They called it "Mount Salubrity." The academy was in a house at the corner of Cummings and John's Road. Lord Sandwich wanted to call the whole community "Salubrity" but Nathaniel Durkee had a self-sufficient plantation called "Summerville." Durkee's pottery was made on the plantation site.

By 1806, the whole Hill settlement had become known as Summerville. Summerville was known for the absence of mosquitoes. They nationally advertised, "No mosquitoes in Summerville." Summerville is some 300 feet above downtown Augusta. With the westerly winds blowing the Hill was more comfortable and healthier than lower Augusta. Early in the 1800s people thought that malaria fever resulted from vapors put off by the river and swamps but Summerville was healthy. Summerville didn't have any fever. Today we know that mosquitoes spread the fever. In 1835 they put in a new road called the "Plank Road." At the bottom of the hill there was a swampy area. The swamp was disrupted when the road was constructed and the mosquitoes moved up to the Hill. Their descendants live in Summerville to this day, biting folks.

Summerville is now a part of the city of Augusta but it wasn't always. The Sand Hills was its own community. In the early 1900s it was too far to drive to Florida for vacation, but the distance to Augusta was just right. The climate in Augusta in the winter was comfortable and hotels, private rooms in homes and even an 18-hole golf course, the Augusta Country

Club, made the area very attractive. The village of Summerville was incorporated in 1861. The city of Augusta had talked about annexation of the Hill for quite some time, but the Hill didn't want to be annexed. At other times Augusta did not want to annex the Hill area. In February of 1910 Dr. Charles W. Hickman was taking his evening stroll up Milledge Road when he was confronted by a person with a pistol and was shot, killed, and robbed. His death was a shock to the community. The residents knew they didn't have enough policemen or fire protection, for that matter. Some of the folks of Summerville then went to Augusta asking for annexation. Augusta approached the State of Georgia gaining approval from the state. A vote was called on October 26, 1911 and 233 people favored annexation and 131 were opposed. On January 1, 1912 annexation took effect. Summerville became the sixth ward of Augusta. Tourism became the cash base in 1921 when the boll weevil wiped out the cotton industry. As someone once said, "tourists went to Summerville, because they were invited." The social season on the Hill was from Thanksgiving to Easter with formal dinner dances being held once or twice a month.

Research resources:

1. *The Story of Augusta. Cashin, Edward J. Spartanburg, SC. The Reprint Company Publishing. (1996)*
2. *Augusta, A Pictorial History. Callahan, Helen. Richmond County Historical Society Publisher. (1980)*
3. *Confederate City, Augusta Georgia 1860-1865. Corley, Florence Fleming. (1995)*
4. Memorial History of Augusta, Georgia. Jones, Charles C. Spartanburg, SC. The Reprint Publishers. (1890)
5. From City to Countryside. Haltermann, Bryan M. (1997)

LUCY CRAFT LANEY

Over the past years many great people have been born or lived in Augusta, Georgia. One such person is the great African American educator, Ms. Lucy Craft Laney. Her name is still on street signs, "Laney Walker Boulevard" and is even the name of a high school. Lucy Laney

was born in Macon, Georgia on April 13, 1854, seven years before the Civil War. Even though it was the time of slavery she was born free, the seventh of ten children. Her parents were the Reverend and Mrs. David Laney. Reverend Laney had purchased his freedom in

1834. He was a Presbyterian minister and was also a quality carpenter, holding side jobs in carpentry to help support his family. He saved enough money so that when he met his wife he could buy her freedom as well. With both parents being free, their children were born free. Lucy

Laney spent her childhood days in Macon where her mother worked as a maid for Ms. Campbell. Many times Lucy would accompany her mother to work. Ms. Campbell noticed how much time little Lucy spent with books and taught Lucy to read at the age of four. She lived in the city of Macon through

the Civil War. When the war came to a close her father rang the bells of Washington Avenue Presbyterian Church to celebrate emancipation. The Freedman's Bureau and the American Missionary Association founded a high school for black children in Macon. Lucy Laney attended the school until she reached the age of fifteen. At that time she was chosen to enroll in the newly founded Atlanta University.

Lucy Craft Laney moved from Macon to attend classes at the new Atlanta University and was a member of the first graduating class in 1873. For the next ten years she traveled around the country teaching. However, it was in Augusta that she found the warmest support for her endeavors. Friends from the Presbyterian Church and the Freedman's Bureau persuaded her to start a school. She began the school in the lecture room of Christ Presbyterian Church with only six children but it soon grew to 200 students. Lucy Laney knew she needed her own building. The Presbyterian churches were having a convention in Minneapolis that year. Lucy only had enough money to go one way, but she went. She boldly approached the convention asking for funds for her school. They told her they didn't have the money but they did buy her a ticket back to Augusta. While she was at the convention she became a good friend of Mrs. P.E.H. Haynes. Mrs. Haynes was president of the women's department of the Presbyterian Church USA. Lucy Laney came back to Augusta and with local support she started building the first building. Then the delayed financial help came from the convention. Mrs. Haynes had become her advocate and supporter. Miss Laney chartered the new school, the "Haynes Normal and Industrial Institute" and educational achievements soon followed. Lucy started the first kindergarten class for black children in Augusta; the first nurses training institute for black girls; and a curriculum that combined traditional arts and sciences with job training. Miss Laney once said, "God has nothing to make men and women of but boys and girls." In 1991, her house on Phillips Street was opened as a museum to the public. Ms. Lucy Craft Laney is buried in front of the school that bears her name - a great educator and a great Georgian.

Research resources:

1. *The Story of Augusta. Cashin, Edward J. Spartanburg, SC. The Reprint Company Publishing. (1996)*
2. *Augusta, A Pictorial History. Callahan, Helen. Richmond County Historical Society Publisher. (1980)*
3. *The Place We Call Home. The Augusta Chronicle*

THE FIRE OF 1916

Augusta from its start has had many ups and downs. For each apparent

Dyer Building

success there seemed to be a failure. The Army Signal Corps opened an airfield and then left; Camp Wheeler closed; the movie industry had betrayed the city; and the city's tallest structure was not yet finished. On March 22, 1916 Augusta's history took a dramatic turn. The downtown area erupted in the worst fire in the city's history. The flames started in the five story Dyer building located on the corner of Jackson (Eighth) and Broad Street. It was believed an unattended iron in the Kelly Dry Goods store caused the fire. The fire started at 6:20 p.m. with the flames being fanned by unusually high winds. The winds took the fire up the elevator shaft which released burning debris down Broad Street toward East Boundary. "I saw things with fire on them as big as my arm just blowing through the air," said Charles B. Whitney Sr., who was a high school senior at the Academy of Richmond County in 1916. "There wasn't any way

Fire of 1916

in the world to stop it." Chief Frank G. Reynolds and Engine Number One were on the scene within minutes, but the fire had already engulfed the five-story building. Burning debris flying through the air landed and started other fires. Chief Reynolds sized up the situation immediately and sent for help from neighboring cities. Assistance came from all around – Macon, Waynesboro, Savannah, Atlanta and even Columbia, South Carolina.

While the help was coming the fire was growing stronger. The winds determined the course of the fire and it went down Jackson to Reynolds, across Jackson and back up to Broad, Ellis and the north side of Greene Street. Many of the city's landmark buildings burned that night: St. Paul's Church, Houghton School, Balk Nursery and Tubman High School just to name a few. The "Cotton Exchange" building lost its roof in the fire, but the building remained in tack. The new "Chronicle Building" and the unfinished "Empire Building" were also gutted. Tom Loyless and the "Augusta Chronicle Newspaper" staff managed to get out a two-page addition on a borrowed press that night. Some of Augusta's finest homes

Fire debris

were lost to the fire but not one person died in the fire. The next day the newspaper said 25 city blocks had been destroyed by the fire. That was later changed to 32 city blocks and 746 buildings. Many warehouses burned, and 20,000 bales of cotton were lost in the blaze. Many of the cotton brokers on cotton row went out of business as their cotton went up in smoke. On the morning of March 23, 3000 people found they were homeless. Many of the people decided to build their homes in the Summerville area leaving their burned-out homes down in the city.

That night Tom Loyless wrote in his "Chronicle" a note of encouragement to the city of Augusta… *"If we know Augustans, and we think we do, Augusta will awake today to a new energy and determination: to rebuild what the flames have destroyed, and to build better before. For be it known, Augusta has faced disasters before…Augusta knows something of adversities and how to overcome them. The lessons she has learned is that reverses test the mettle of cities as they do of men: that obstacles spur us to greater effort and determination and that the surest and quickest way to overcome a loss is to begin at once to repair it. So let's all join in bright and early this morning: wash the smoke off our faces, shake the cinders off our clothes– wade right in to show what old Augusta really can do when she tries."*

William H. Barrett was named by city Mayor James R. Littleton to head a public safety committee of 15 citizens. Within 10 minutes Barrett was promised $10,000 for immediate relief for the suffering. The Chronicle ran a front page list of the whereabouts of more than 80 families displaced by the fire. Railroad companies offered free transportation to people who had lost everything in the fire and wanted to return to former out-of-town residences. Even though he lost his office in the Chronicle building and his home, Barrett contributed substantially to the relief fund himself. Over $63,000 was received and distributed. Barrett concluded his final report with the words, *"in this great disaster our people have measured fully up to their best traditions, and nobly illustrated how their virtues can be as great as their distresses."*

St. Paul's was rebuilt on the same site. It looked the same as before but was rebuilt a little larger. The Chronicle and Empire buildings were gutted but structurally sound so they would be restored. A new Houghton School was constructed. Tubman High School was moved to the Schuetzenplatz property and rebuilt. The downtown residents constructed slowly over the next two decades, reflecting a depressed economy and changing the face of Augusta. Fortunately, most of Greene Street and parts of Telfair remained to remind us of the elegance of old Augusta.

On December 30, 1916 the beautiful Hampton Terrace Hotel in North Augusta was destroyed by fire. The Chief of Firefighters was asked if Augusta could burn like it did in the 1916 fire. He confidently answered no, because buildings are built differently today.

Research resources:
1. *The Story of Augusta. Cashin, Edward J. Spartanburg, SC. The Reprint Company Publishing. (1996)*
2. *The Place We Call Home. The Augusta Chronicle (1997)*

Made in the USA
Columbia, SC
31 October 2020